A Story
That Had To Be Told

*The challenges and triumphs of an
extraordinary Chicago woman*

J G Jung

iUniverse, Inc.
New York   Bloomington

A Story That Had To Be Told

The challenges and triumphs of an extraordinary Chicago woman

iUniverse books may be ordered through booksellers or by contacting:

iUniverse
1663 Liberty Drive
Bloomington, IN 47403
www.iuniverse.com
1-800-Authors (1-800-288-4677)

ISBN: 978-0-595-52653-6 (pbk)
ISBN: 978-0-595-51625-4 (cloth)
ISBN: 978-0-595-62707-3 (ebk)

Printed in the United States of America

Contents

The story of Andrea's life is dedicated to anyone who has experienced the depths of despair and felt a sense of overwhelming hopelessness. To find oneself having hit bottom in the middle of life is a shuddering experience. Refusing to give up and having the courage to look for hope when none may exist is truly a gift.

Foreword

Experiences in life are nearly always connected to each other in some way. Without any one of those experiences, we could not have arrived at where we are. One event leads to another, and yet another, all leading us to new people, new places, and new experiences. These are the links of our lives. Some experiences are soon forgotten until future events draws memories of them to the surface. Other experiences are forgotten completely, but really never relinquish their power to influence how we see the world and how we react to it. While still other experiences seem to define our lives, either: 'making or breaking' us. In other words, for most of us the events in our lives determine who we are, what we do, and how we see the world.

Throughout our lives many of us may be fortunate enough to have known an individual for whom these rules do not apply. Just every now and then we may come to know someone who decides for themselves how the events in life will affect them. They decide what lessons are to be learned. They don't allow society to tell them what they are capable of or what they can achieve. They don't think in terms of 'odds' or 'percentages' or 'plausibility'. They take life as it comes and work with what they have.

They don't judge themselves, nor do they judge others. They believe that people are basically good and when given the choice most people will do the right thing. They never feel as though they have to protect themselves from other people or safeguard themselves from future events. They generally like more people than they dislike. And as a consequence, they have more friends than most people. This is a story of such an individual.

A life-long Chicagoan now in her mid-seventies, Andrea's life is an example of the courage and potential which lies within all of us. Even in her darkest days in the middle of her life, she somehow managed to find a way through, when a way out would have ended her pain more quickly. Surviving what she had endured would have been nearly impossible for many of us. Transcending her circumstance to achieve the unthinkable would surely have been impossible for all but a precious few. In some ways, she did the only thing she could do. But Andrea doesn't see it that way. She sees her life as the way it needed to be, as a journey that she wouldn't change for all the money or comfort in the world. Andrea reflects on her life with only joy and a sense of enlightenment. When asked about an extremely painful and difficult part of her life, she will not recall the hopelessness or desperation, but only the good that came from it and what she learned about herself in the process. She can only see the good in the world and the good in others. This is the true story of one woman's unwillingness to give up on herself and her family.

The Anniversary

✦

October 2004

People who live in Chicago wait anxiously for the coming of spring. Winters are long, windy, and cold. When spring finally arrives a sense of relief puts most everyone there in a good mood. Chicago is a place of unpredictable weather. The old saying is, 'if you don't like the weather in Chicago, stick around for ten more minutes.' The temperature changes from hot to cold or from beautiful to miserable without a moment's notice. So beautiful days are cherished, no matter what time of year it happens to be.

If spring is anxiously awaited, then autumn is savored. Few actually look forward to autumn for the simple reason that they know winter is right behind it. There is sadness to the passing of another summer, because sometimes Chicagoans question if they can make it through another long and grueling winter. But autumn in Chicago is breathtaking. It feels a bit like the weather in southern California, only with the big oak and maple trees displaying their brilliant colors along the side streets and in the city parks. The humidity, so typical of Chicago summers evaporates into cool, crisp mornings and golden red sunset skies. It might best be described as invigorating.

The day of the ceremony was in fact a perfect autumn day. Planning for their 50th wedding anniversary had begun well in advance of the actual anniversary. Discussions about how and where they would celebrate that day went on for months. It is hard to underestimate the importance that this anniversary had for Don and Andrea. It was in a sense, confirmation that they had done something right. Even with everything that had been thrown at them during their fifty years of marriage, they had survived it all, good, bad, and everything in between. And they survived it all together.

Many of their close friends, most of them actually, had not made it this far. Either the husband had died, which was usually the case, or in some instances the wife had passed away. In still others, both had died. They had even witnessed a divorce or two. Some of their friends had moved away, while others hit it big and traded their energies previously spent on maintaining relationships for the all-consuming task of figuring out ways to best spend their money. They had lost friends through disagreements and irreconcilable differences in values too. But their friends that had made it, and were still close to them, were cherished. Don and Andrea had always enjoyed authentic, interesting, and honest people.

It was important that all their children be there to celebrate their 50th wedding anniversary. It would be a challenge of course, because their five children were spread out throughout the country. Four of the kids had children of their own. Because of busy schedules, financial constraints, and all the responsibilities in raising their families, it would require a lot of advanced planning to have all the kids in the same place at the same time. Quite a lot of coordination was required to pull this off, so Andrea took control of the effort and began the process more than a year before the event.

Andrea and Don were married back in 1954 at Our Lady of Mount Carmel on Belmont Avenue near the lake. They decided to renew their vows at that very same church, in essence, to get married again. So Andrea called to reserve the church on the exact date of their anniversary. They hadn't stepped foot in that church since their wedding day.

Andrea's original wedding dress was still in her possession. For 50 years it had been stored in a cedar chest in her house. She had saved it for posterity, not thinking that she would ever wear it again in public. But when she took the dress out and tried it on, to her surprise, it fit. It had a few of the original stains still on it from the wedding fifty years before, but that was of no concern. She decided that she would wear that same dress for the anniversary ceremony. Word of this spread among the women in the family and before long, two more of the original dresses worn at the wedding were found. The maid of honor's dress that her cousin and friend Dolores had worn was pulled out of retirement. That dress would be worn by Andrea's original flower girl, who was now in her fifties. One of Andrea's three daughters wore one of the other original dresses. Three original vintage dresses being worn at a 50th anniversary, at the same church, on the exact same day, actually made it into the local paper. It was a welcome added bit of attention to the event that made Andrea that much more excited.

All the kids were there and had come from all over the country. One came in from the eastern most Midwest, one from the Southwest, another from the Southeast, and the two youngest who were in the Chicago area. Although their children's spouses couldn't come for some scheduling and financial reasons, everyone from Don and Andrea's immediate family was there. Of course, only a handful of those present at their wedding in 1954 were there because Don and Andrea had outlived ninety-nine percent of them. The two of them were there, and that was what was important. It was a day they had anticipated for a long time.

It was an emotional time for the whole family. Their kids had rarely been in the same place at the same time for some time, so they had a chance to catch up with one another and reminisce. Before the ceremony started the kids were able to explore the empty church and recall stories about their parents and their days as children together. Don and Andrea had been together long enough and had lived long enough to pass a threshold few are able to enjoy, fifty years together. Standing on the altar, dressed as if they were to be married for the first time with their children and close friends in attendance, was a once in a lifetime experience for both of them. Nobody present was able to fight back the tears as they renewed their vows that day. Don had rarely been seen crying in public, not unlike most men, but on this day the tears were streaming down his face.

The church itself hadn't changed in a half a century. The organ was just as imposing as it was so long ago, having been recently restored. The soaring ceiling was no less impressive and the stained glass windows were all as they were. They exited the church and found themselves on the same granite staircase where they stood fifty years before on the doorstep of a new life together, the twin limestone spires adorning the façade still stood behind them. But now they stood there with a half a century having gone by, and the majority of their life together having passed. Both Don and Andrea were surprised in a way, surprised that they had made it. It was all worth it though, without a doubt. All of their kids were alive and well. They had done their job, imperfectly yes, but done it nonetheless. As they walked down the front stairs of the church, the cars passing by were honking away, just as they had when they first stood on those steps. There were four hundred people in attendance at their wedding in 1954, but today there was only a dozen or so. But that was fine because anyone who meant something to them and were still alive were there, for the most part anyway.

It was an exhausting and emotional day that signaled the passing of another milestone and the start of the rest of their lives together. They went back to their regular routine, taking rides together up Sheridan Road and going out for lunch. More and more doctor's visits worked their way into their schedule as their advancing age made it increasingly obvious that their healthiest years were behind them. Even with mounting health issues, Andrea was really enjoying this time in her life, and so was Don.

By her own admission Andrea had made it to this point in her life as a result of positive thinking and never giving up. It seemed that the events of years past would prevent her from being here, but she truly believes that everything happens for a reason. Her life had begun more than seventy years before during a much different time and her journey has been an inspiration to all who know her. Whatever life-shattering events may come along, there inevitably exist a ray of light somewhere within our reach. No matter how insurmountable challenges and setbacks may seem, hope can be found if you just keep looking.

Like so many Americans, Andrea was a child of immigrants. To tell Andrea's story it is important to introduce you to the people who brought her into this world. To do that we have to go back to a very different time when the 19th century was giving way to a new century, and America was on the threshold of incredible changes. This was a time before automobiles and electricity, telephones and highways, and just about everything else that we take for granted today.

Daughter of Immigrants

✦

Andrea's father was born Louis Schenk in Gelsenkirchen, Germany in 1900. Gelsenkirchen was the most important coal mining town in Europe at the time. It was known as *the city of a thousand fires*, referring to the flames of mine gasses flaring during the night. Louis' father worked in the coal mines there. His parents immigrated to America in 1901, bringing with them their children, Louis included. They had followed many other German immigrants to work in the coal mines in and around Pittsburg, Kansas. At the time there were some fifty coal companies employing more than 11,000 men in Pittsburg.

Louis' father gained employment in a coal mine in Pittsburg where he worked for seventeen years. It was a bleak and difficult way of life, but better than what they had back home in Germany. The family of seven was able to rent a small farm house with plenty of outdoor space to grow vegetables. It was better than life in a tenement in the city, plus Louis' father knew coal mining.

The great flu epidemic of 1918 claimed his father's life, as it did hundreds of thousands of other Americans in the months following the return of our soldiers from the battlefields of Europe after the end of the Great War. Two days before his father died, he came home from the mines very ill and said 'I'm going to lie down and I will never get up again.' He never did get up again and died at home. But Louis wasn't there for his father's death. He was already gone.

At the young age of fifteen, Louis hopped on a freight train, left Kansas, and headed west. He was in search of opportunity, adventure, and the legendary sights of the great American west. It was easy to board a freight train in Pittsburg because it was located at the junction of four major railway systems, so the trains had to stop there. A fifteen year old taking off like that in today's world would surely trigger a missing persons report, but it was different back then. Notwithstanding that Louis was in fact a habitual runaway. He would leave home and disappear for weeks, even months on end, leaving his parents to wonder of his fate. Finally, when he was fifteen, his parents threw him out of the house, along with at least one of his brothers, and told them to fend for themselves. So that is exactly what Louis did.

In those days, according to Louis, it was easy to travel across the country. All you had to do was go to the railroad office, sign up as a brakeman and work until you arrived at the next stop, which was some 200-300 miles away, collect your pay and quit. He found employment in places like Buffalo Wyoming, Butte Montana, and Fresno California. It was during these days that Louis' love for the West was born, a love that he would eventually pass down to his daughter, Andrea. His journeys took him from the deserts of Arizona to the Canadian Rockies and eventually back east, all the way to New York City, where he gained employment as a window washer on a high rise apartment building. It was there in New York in the midst of the 'roaring twenties' where Louis met his future wife and Andrea's mother. Her name was Andrea too.

Louis was a strong and self-reliant individual that believed if you want something done, you have to do it yourself. His friends called him 'Red', because he had a full head of red hair. In his later years it turned to pure white. He was always fit and very strong. Louis' strength and capacity to withstand adversity were passed on to Andrea, and that fortitude would serve her well throughout her life. Andrea always spoke of her father with a great deal of affection. He had always treated her with respect and consideration. Louis would live into his 83rd year in near perfect health. A pulmonary disorder finally took his life.

Her mother was born in Marne, Germany in the same year as her father, 1900. Her name was Andrea Augusta Maria Voss and was the youngest of eleven children. She seldom spoke of her childhood or hometown. She used to say, *'I don't like to think of those bad memories.'* As a teenager, she moved to Hamburg, where she gained employment as a housekeeper for a local baron. Not much else is known of her mother's life in the old country, she simply never spoke of it.

In 1926, she came to America aboard the S.S. Resolute from Hamburg, with her half brother Otto and they settled in New York City. There she worked as a housekeeper and Otto worked as a tailor. While visiting Otto one day near his tailor shop on Long Island, she met Louis. The two married only three weeks later in 1927.

Once married, Louis and his wife moved into a building on west 70th Street, where they traded their maintenance services for free rent. They lived there from 1927 to 1932. When the Great Depression began to take hold of the country, the two left New York and headed to Chicago, where Louis' brother Dave lived with his wife. But jobs were scarce there too, so Louis left his wife in Chicago while he headed west again, in search of opportunity. Eventually Louis returned to Chicago after nearly a year of bad luck on the road, and made Chicago their home.

They lived in Chicago until 1966 when Louis retired, and then spent their final days together in a small retirement village in Hot Springs, Arkansas. Louis passed on in 1983, and his wife in 1989. During the 56 years of their married life, Louis never spoke fluent German, and his wife never spoke fluent English.

Our story begins in a north side Chicago neighborhood during the height of the Great Depression. Andrea was the daughter of immigrant parents who sought to provide for her a decent and respectable way of life. In that regard, young Andrea was no different from so many countless others during those days.

The Early Years

✦

Hard times had come to America. The waves of immigrants who had arrived in America prior to the stock market crash of 1929 had seen their hope of a better life fading away. Jobs and opportunity were vanishing, and families struggled to support themselves. Unemployment was at its highest level in all of American history. Breadlines and panhandlers were as common a sight as the desperation on the faces of those who were hardest hit. Parents provided for their children and themselves as best they could. People did anything they had to in order to make ends meet. Nothing went to waste.

She was born Andrea Schenk in the spring of 1934 at Chicago Memorial Hospital in the midst of the Great Depression. Andrea's mother would tell her in later years that she could see the World's Fair from the hospital room window. That World's Fair (1933-1934) gave Chicagoans some badly needed jobs, but also gave them hope for the future. The World's Fair would eventually come to a close, leaving Chicago and its people to struggle their way through the remaining years of the Depression. No one knew just how long it would last, nor did they know that World War II was looming on the horizon. World War I, known as the Great War and the war to end all wars, had ended just sixteen years before in 1918.

Very few people in the city owned their own homes. They had to rent apartments, or flats that were available to them. In some cases, people lived in rooming houses, with cramped living quarters and community bathrooms. Other families who were hardest hit by the collapsing economy were less fortunate. Having no options, many uprooted themselves and headed west, looking for any work they could find. For these people, well at least for the adults, the exuberance of the 1920's seemed like a dream that had somehow slipped away. As for the children, this was all they knew. And for Andrea, this was all she knew. But Andrea's parents always provided for her. She never went hungry, and always felt safe.

The Schenks took Andrea home to a basement apartment on Chicago's north side, near North Avenue and Halsted Street. But the Public Health nurse told the Schenks that the low light conditions in a basement apartment would be bad for young Andrea's eyes. So the family moved to a rooming house with a first floor, well-lit flat on BellePlaine Street. Although her family shared a community bathroom with the other residents, and other inconveniences associated with community living, it would be better for Andrea's health.

Three months after Andrea was born, her mother unknowingly found herself a witness to a legendary event in Chicago history. It was the night of July 22, 1934. It was 109 degrees in Chicago that day, and many north-siders headed to find relief from the heat at the Biograph Theater. This was because the Biograph was one of the few 'air-cooled' or air-conditioned buildings of that time. Her husband walked her to the theater so that she could watch the Manhattan Melodrama and cool down. It was a bit too extravagant for both of them to buy a ticket to see the movie, so Louis dropped her off. When the movie ended, she met with her husband out front to learn that the infamous gangster, John Dillinger, had just been shot and killed in the alley adjacent to the theater. Andrea's mother retold this story throughout her life. But it was surely a sign of the times. In that same year, 1934, Charles 'Pretty Boy' Floyd was shot and killed by federal agents on a farm in Ohio. George 'Baby Face' Nelson was found dead in a roadside ditch outside Chicago. And Bonnie and Clyde were ambushed and killed by authorities in Louisiana. It was the end of an era.

In 1935 the Schenks finally got the financial break they needed. Under President Roosevelt, the Works Progress Administration was formed to help ease the financial suffering of unemployed or under employed Americans. The WPA would give men $50 a month in a 'security wage', for which they in turn would build roads and bridges, creating America's new infrastructure. Louis worked on the lakefront project, creating the park system built on landfill, on Chicago's north side. That job was a Godsend for the Schenks. It put food on the table, but more important, gave them hope for the future. Things were looking up.

It was at the rooming house on BellePlaine that Andrea's little brother Bob was born in 1936. Andrea always loved and appreciated her little brother, as he did her. They would remain close friends all of Bob's life. The Schenk's family was now complete.

The rooming house on BellePlaine would also provide Andrea with her first traumatic experience in the form of a fall. It was a first floor flat with an open porch off the kitchen. One day she was jumping up and down on a cot next to the railing and fell over to the ground below. She was four years old. Everything seemed fine immediately after the fall, at least for a while. But later on in the middle of the night, she woke up hemorrhaging from her lungs. Her father quickly carried her down to a neighbor's car and they took her to Children's Memorial Hospital. To this day, she remembers sitting on her father's lap in the car, coughing up huge chunks of blood. That was all she remembers. In later years she learned that she didn't recognize anyone for the first three weeks after the fall, and was in the hospital for nearly three months. But she eventually recovered. Nearly seventy years later, Andrea would again find herself coughing up chunks of blood.

In 1939 the family moved to an apartment on Dakin Street where Andrea attended kindergarten at The Stewart School. One of Andrea's fondest memories during that time was Halloween. Her mother made her a costume out of whatever they had available. She recalls how beautiful she felt wearing that costume. She always loved to dress up, especially for Halloween.

Andrea loved to take walks with her father. She asked him all the time and he would more often than not grant her request. Andrea remembers walking alongside as Louis pushed little Bob's buggy. They would walk past the pumping station on Montrose Avenue, under the viaduct and to the Peace Garden on the lakefront. The Peace Garden had a waterfall and an eagle made of stone perched on top. It was a part of the same lakefront project where Louis had been employed.

As for all kids her age, this was a time of curiosity and exploration. Everything was a wonder to her. She remembers her fascination watching a golden brown caterpillar crawl up her arm that she had found on a mulberry tree near her house. But as for most of us, our early childhood memories become increasingly harder to recall as the years pass. So only a few of her memories from that time have survived.

In 1940 they moved to another apartment on Reta Street. Louis paid $25 a month for rent for the third floor flat. It was there where the family stayed and called home. Andrea lived the rest of her youth there, only leaving to marry in 1954. The flat had five rooms, which was a much larger living area than the Schenks were used to. But it didn't have the conveniences the family would enjoy in later years. The family's clothes had to be washed on a scrub board in the bath tub, and then hung in the third floor front hallway to dry. Hot water for bathing had to be heated first, and then poured into the tub. On cold nights, Andrea's mother would heat up bricks in the stove, wrap them in towels, and put them in bed with the kids to keep them warm. Andrea also remembers waking up on those cold mornings and scraping the ice off the windows to see if it had snowed the night before. Although it may seem to some as a difficult way to live, so many others were far worse off, and the Schenks knew it. This was their home and they loved living there. The hot water heater, washing machine, radio, and television set would eventually come, but not just yet.

Andrea attended LeMoyne grammar school, which was one of the best schools in that area and only a block away from their apartment. It was so close that she could hear the school bell ring from the apartment window. This is where she met many of her lifelong friends and had her best memories.

Bob and Andrea had their chores on Reta Street. Andrea would clean the hallway, all the way down to the first floor every Saturday. Bob was responsible for taking the trash out to the alley. When Bob left without taking the trash, his father would wait until he was all the way at the bottom of the stairs, and call him back. Bob learned his lesson and always remembered the trash from then on.

One can never predict what events or memories early in life will have lasting effects on someone. In fourth grade Andrea had to draw a picture to be presented to her parents on parents' night. She drew beautiful flowers with a black background so that the flowers would stand out. She had put a lot of effort and care into that picture and was very proud of it. She was expecting praise. But her teacher frowned on the picture and said that it wasn't very good, suggesting that Andrea do it over. The teacher's reaction offended Andrea enough that she could instantly recall decades later how it affected her. It made her feel like she wasn't good enough. As a result, years would pass before she would draw again. That experience resurfaced later in Andrea's life when she set out on a journey of self discovery.

By this time, her father had gained employment with the Chicago Northwestern Railroad as a Brakeman. The Schenks were now enjoying some financial stability. They weren't well off by any means, but they now had a steady income and life began to get better. Louis spent the rest of his working life on the railroad, in one position or another. It was that stability in the 'cold water' flat on Reta Street that Andrea remembers. Those were good times for her. When she speaks of her youth there, it always brings a warm smile to her face.

Life was a bit more fun for the children of that time. They were allowed to just be kids. There were no pressures, no personal electronics or video games, and no busy schedules to keep. After school they would come home to their chores, and then find ways to entertain themselves. Andrea recalls sitting on the front stoop with the other children and just talking. They also played hopscotch and skipped rope on the sidewalk and played marbles in the dirt. It was a simpler time.

In 1945, the year the war in Europe and the South Pacific was ending; Louis loaded Andrea and Bob onto a train, and headed to Kansas. Louis loved to take his family to the places he knew as a young man. Because he worked for the railroad, the fares were cheap. He took the kids to Kansas to meet his sister, who still lived there. Andrea remembers the ride because the train was filled with soldiers returning from Europe. She felt rather special, being in their presence, with their uniforms and all. As far as she was concerned, those soldiers had saved the world. They were heroes. When she searches for memories of World War II, this is what she recalls.

The years on Reta Street provided Andrea with the foundation of her personality and her character. Her unfailing trust in others was instilled in her at this time, beginning with her mother. In later years she wrote,

'I believe my high level of trust for others came from a strong foundation in infancy, of a good, kind, and loving mother who would never abandon me.'

But there were others who taught Andrea that people were essentially good and to always look for the good in others. Living directly across the street from the Schenks was one of those people. Her name was Mrs. Ramage. She was in her eighties at the time, which would put her actual birth date sometime just before the Civil War. Mrs. Ramage was the oldest person Andrea had ever seen at that point in her life. She had white hair and always sat in a chair in her living room. Andrea never saw her stand. She treated Andrea with kindness and spoke to her as if she were a daughter of her own. Andrea would bring chicken soup over to her when there was extra. She spoke more openly to Andrea than Andrea's mother was able to because of her mother's broken English. She treated her like Andrea was her daughter, taking her under her wing in a sense. There were others too. Older women in the neighborhood who loved to talk to Andrea and give her little gifts and things. From that time forward Andrea admired older people, and felt that there was a lot to learn from them. Throughout her life she went out of her way to be especially respectful of the elderly. In her later years, Andrea would dedicate all her time to support and assist senior citizens, even when she was a senior citizen herself.

Andrea sees her life as a series of links that connect one event in her life to another. In seventh grade, she and her classmates were invited to her teacher's wedding. The children that attended all hopped on the Broadway Avenue street car and rode it to Devon Avenue and then west to the old St. Henry's church. She didn't know it at the time, but this church would eventually become the parish which she would belong to for more than fifty years. She recalls that it seemed as if they were so far away. Andrea had never traveled that far on the red street car before, even though it was just a few miles away. Throughout her youth she never forgot that place, especially the long purple drapes hanging inside the church. She would see those curtains again, shortly after she met her future husband some ten years later.

Now Andrea's parents weren't churchgoing people, although, they did feel that religious education and understanding would be good for their daughter. So every Sunday, Andrea, along with other kids from the neighborhood, would attend services at a nearby church. A bus would pick up the kids in the morning and drop them back off at home in the late afternoon. This went on for a year or more. Then one Sunday after arriving at the church, Andrea found that the service had changed under the direction of a new minister. It was now what is referred to as *charismatic.* She sat in the church and watched the congregation speaking *in tongue.* They were chanting and crying and screaming. The sight of this behavior literally terrified her. She was shaken and frightened, and never returned. Years went by before she would see such a thing again. And when she did, it would trigger that fear she felt as a child and have disastrous results.

Eventually she attended a few services at Our Lady of Mount Carmel on Belmont Avenue. Andrea didn't actually convert to Catholicism until she met her future husband, but attended mass occasionally with her cousin nonetheless. Andrea would of course marry at that very same church a decade or so later and of course celebrate her 50th wedding anniversary there as well. But she had much to endure before then.

An Adventure to Remember

✦

Summer of 1947/1948
World War II had ended and the troops had come home.
There had been much anxiety throughout the nation that
the hard times of the 1930's would return following the war.
But to the delight of the nation the opposite occurred. The
economy was entering a boom not seen since the 1920's. The
GI Bill sent the returning troops off to college and out into
the working world. Seemingly endless suburban residential
developments were under construction throughout the
country to house a new generation of heroes and their
young families. There was exuberance in the air as hope and
opportunity returned to a nation that had a new sense of
pride and a feeling of self-confidence. People from all over
America loaded up their automobiles and set out to see the
country. The Schenks were no different.

In 1947, Andrea's mom and dad took her and her little
brother Bob on an adventure of a lifetime. This is another
important link in her life. Her father Louis took the family

to see the magnificent sights of the great American West, the same sights he saw as a young man. Andrea always spoke of this time in her life with a gleam in her eye and a swollen heart. These memories remained as vivid for Andrea as any over the years.

Louis had purchased a 1935 Ford specifically to take the family out west. The winter before their 1947 trip, he dismantled the Ford, literally down to the frame, and rebuilt it. All the worn parts were replaced and everything else was sanded and painted before going back on the car. He modified the interior to accommodate the family's sleeping arrangements, and built a carryall for the roof of the car to store their belongings. This was something he had wanted to do for many years.

Years later Andrea wrote down her experiences to hand down to her children so those memories would never be lost. She describes the vacation of a lifetime in her own words:

'We packed up our 1935 Ford, shut off the gas and electric at home, and we were on our way! Dad took a two-month leave of absence from the railroad and we headed out west. It was his dream to take mom and show her the country but was unable to do it in the 1930's because of the Depression. Now he had two extra passengers, Bob and me. Our first trip was in 1947, Bob was ten and I was thirteen years old. We had no camp stove, no tent or lantern, just our trusty 'old faithful', the 1935 Ford. We traveled ten thousand miles each vacation and never had a flat tire. We never ate in a restaurant or stayed in a motel on either vacation.

Gasoline was twenty-one cents a gallon. Our traveling expenses for two months were $250.00. Dad usually didn't drive more than 45 miles per hour and two hundred miles a day. When late afternoon came he would look for a quiet spot, *hopefully near a stream, river, or small lake, and we would settle in for the night.*

Bob and I would gather kindling wood and Dad would build a fire for our evening meal. He made a makeshift stove from a grate that sat on four metal legs. If Dad caught fish that was our dinner. Mom and I would clean up after dinner and Dad and Bob would prepare the car for sleeping. The two front seats were unhinged and placed outside the car. A mattress which was stored in the carrying box on top of the car was placed on the floor inside. If the weather was good, I would sleep outside on an army cot next to the car, Mom would sleep on the back seat, Dad and Bob were on the floor. If it rained, I slept inside on the floor.

Whenever we saw a nice campground, we would stay there. In Big Sur, California, the campground was so nice that we stayed for ten days. They had showers and washing machines for the clothes, even cabinets to put dishes in. My favorite states were South Dakota, Wyoming, Montana, Idaho, Washington, Oregon, California, Arizona, Utah, and Colorado. Special attractions were the Black Hills, Yellowstone Park, Glacier Park, Columbia River Drive, Crater Lake, Mt. Ranier, Mt. Hood, the Redwoods, Carmel, San Francisco, Yosemite, the Grand Canyon, Zion National Park, Bryce Canyon, and the Gunnison River.

The following year we had a Coleman stove, a gas lantern, and a tent. We were living. It's difficult to pick out one special place that was memorable, but the one that was beautiful and interesting that immediately comes to mind is in Montana. We found a beautiful out of the way campground called Bowman Lake in Glacier National Park. We pitched our tent near the Flathead River and set up camp. Dad, and Bob and I decided to hike on a trail. We walked for about a quarter of a mile and came upon a large clearing. In the clearing was a large log cabin with smoke coming out of the chimney. As we approached the cabin, we noticed the grass in this huge clearing looked like it had been mowed. Two men came out. The older man was in his seventies and the younger man around sixty-five.

The two men homesteaded this beautiful piece of land before Glacier became a National Park, which was in 1918. They were allowed to shoot deer for their food. The two men were happy to have visitors and we sat and enjoyed the wonderful stories they shared. They came by covered wagon around 1912. We were offered coffee and homemade bread which the older man made himself in a huge wood-burning cast iron stove. We stayed at Bowman Lake Campground for almost ten days. Dad and I would catch rainbow trout and give it to the old men and they would give us fresh vegetables from their garden.

The reason the huge clearing looked like it had been mowed was because of rabbits. We were told that someone gave the men two rabbits a couple of years earlier and now hundreds of rabbits kept the grass mowed.

One day Bob and I went down to the river to play in the water. A young man who lived nearby came down to talk to us. He invited us into his cabin by the river. This is where I had my first peanut butter and jelly sandwich. He played his guitar and sang to us. These were very special memories.'

That same man took quite a liking to Andrea. He and Andrea actually corresponded by mail in the months after their vacation. Finally he sent a letter asking her to marry him and move out west. She responded by informing him that she couldn't marry him because she was only 14 years old. She never heard from him again.

Young Adulthood

✦

There were few children, at least the children of immigrants that received an allowance of any kind. All the income that came into the household was used sparingly, because memories of the hardships of the Depression and the war were still fresh in their minds. Kids would often take jobs after school to help the family or provide themselves with a few extra dollars for entertainment. Andrea worked a variety of odd jobs for that purpose. Working also provided young adults understanding of the value of a dollar.

Her first job was as a babysitter for a dollar a day. She also worked as a waitress in a small restaurant, at a local dry cleaner, a dime store, and small factory for 75 cents an hour. She didn't like the factory job at all, and consequently it didn't last very long. And then the carnival came to town.

The carnival would come to the city every summer. Andrea and her cousin Dolores were able to get jobs at the carnival. Traveling carnivals have lost much of their importance over the years. These days, the carnival has taken a back seat to other forms of modern entertainment, but in those days, the carnival was a real treat. The lights and sounds and activity of a carnival were exciting and an annual delight for the local community. Carnivals were so popular that they had evolved into permanent amusement parks, as was the case with Riverview Amusement Park, at Belmont and Western. Giant amusement parks would eventually appear across the country as the natural successor to this form of entertainment which had planted its roots in 19th century America. But the spectacle of a traveling show goes much further back in time in Europe and elsewhere. Andrea describes working at the carnival:

'During the summer of 1949 and 1950, Dolores and I worked for a carnival which traveled around the city and to Gary, Indiana. We met Flo and her husband when their carnival was in an empty lot not too far from our home. Flo was looking for workers to work in various game booths. She paid us $5.00 each night and made sure we were brought right to our house in the evening after the carnival closed, which was around midnight. We loved our first big paying job. Our parents were promised she would always take us home, and she did.'

The girls had a great time in their youth. Kids love to explore and they did just that. The two would occasionally hop on the bus for the five-cent fare and ride it all day. The bus would take them down to the loop and then out to the end of the line at Cumberland Ave, and then back again. Oftentimes, the conductor wouldn't take a second fare from the girls for the return trip home, providing them with a five-cent, daylong tour of the city.

Andrea had another good friend besides her cousin Dolores. Her name was Pat. She had always told Andrea, throughout their lifelong friendship, that Andrea was the nicest person she knew. They both attended Lake View High School. Pat lived close to Andrea and they found themselves always hanging out together. In high school Pat worked at a local movie theater. Andrea and Pat's boyfriend, Loring, sat through quite a few movies there, waiting for Pat to get off of work. Pat made sure that Andrea and Loring got their fair share of free popcorn too. Loring attended Lane Tech High School, so dances at Lane Tech High School and basketball games were common, thanks to Loring. It was an exciting time in Andrea's life, meeting new people and exploring the city.

'*After school, in our junior year, Pat worked as a candy girl in a theater. Loring and I would meet her there, sit and watch the movie until Pat finished work, then we would come home together. The very first time I felt glamorous was when Loring took me to his bowling banquet. Pat couldn't go for one reason or another, so he took me. I had a black dress on with baby doll high heels that had ankle straps. He whirled me around the dance floor. It was memorable evening. I was sixteen years old.*'

A Love for a Lifetime

✦

Andrea was a beautiful young woman. She was about five feet six inches tall with wavy golden brown hair and bright hazel eyes. A voluptuous figure and a contagious smile made her quite the catch for some lucky boy. Her romantic life started during her employment at a north side grocery store called The National Tea. This part of her life is certainly the most memorable for her. She was coming of age. Andrea hadn't started dating yet, but she was about to, and in a big way.

She worked as a checker at the National Tea on Irving Park and Broadway. She always said hello to the milkman who came to the store every week to deliver milk, his name was John. Andrea had no idea that John had a son. This is where the next chapter in Andrea's life begins.

'I was behind the cash register at the National Tea. I looked up and there he was, the man I would spend the rest of my life with. He was pushing cases full of milk on a dolly into the store. He smiled at me and I smiled back. I thought maybe this good-looking, strong young man might be John's son, but I wasn't sure.

What really attracted me was his smile. When the milk was all delivered he left without saying anything. That evening he called my Aunt Anne's house. She yelled up the gangway and I ran down to get the call. It was him. He introduced himself and said he was John's son. His name was Don.

He asked if I would like to go out the next day, which happened to be my day off. I said yes, of course. I had turned seventeen two months earlier. He was twenty. Don and I hit it off right from the beginning. He picked me up in his Dad's 1951 Oldsmobile Super 88. It was black and shiny. I had never gone out with anyone with a car, except for Loring. We took a drive up Sheridan Road along the north shore. It was a Tuesday.

We stopped up at Plaza Del Lago when there were very few buildings there. There was a small ice cream shop on the east side of Sheridan Road that was where I had my very first milk shake. Don had a blow-up raft and we went to the beach near Winnetka. He blew up the raft and asked if I wanted to go out. I went out only a short way and became afraid because I didn't know how to swim. We had a good time anyway. The next day he picked me up after work and we went out for a couple of hours. That was the beginning of seeing each other almost every night.'

Andrea was beaming with excitement at this time in her life. When she smiled, as Don would later say, she smiled with her whole body. She was physically attractive, very sexy, good-looking, and outgoing. She had a natural attraction that anyone who met her took notice of immediately. Don was physically strong and well built, having played four years of high school football. Handsome, well spoken, and polite, he seemed to be the perfect match for Andrea. When the two were together they were indeed the 'all American' young couple. It could be said that they epitomized health, youth, and the excitement of being young and in love. Anyone who saw them together knew that they would eventually marry.

It was the early 1950's and Chicago and the country were entering a time of economic expansion not seen in more than a generation. The young people were coming of age during a time of affluence never experienced in America before, and the exuberance was tangible. These were the 'happy days' of American history. Big, beautiful, and luxurious automobiles, diners and dances, milkshakes and music, these were their times. Hair was getting longer, skirts were getting shorter, and the music was getting faster and louder. Rock and roll had exploded on to the scene. And for the first time in more than a quarter of a century, people had expendable income. Everyone's hopes were so high. What a time it was to be young. This is when Don and Andrea came of age. They didn't challenge authority like some, but this was their time nevertheless. Their decision to 'go along' with authority would create dire challenges down the road, but not yet. They were young and in love. Oh how sweet it was.

'We were both attracted to each other from the moment our eyes met. He was so different from anyone I knew. For me, it was love at first sight. Don was curious to see who I was because it was the first time his father commented on any girl. Don felt that he didn't have a chance with me. His feeling was that I must have had a lot going for me with other friends in my life.

I was treated like a queen. Don was always polite, caring, attentive to me, and planned our 'get togethers' so we would both enjoy ourselves. Right from the beginning we both enjoyed just taking a ride in the car, stopping for a milkshake or breaded shrimp at the Fish Keg on Howard Street. This form of dating has continued through our entire married life. We still enjoy our rides.'

Andrea and Don still take their rides up Sheridan Road along the lake. This tradition has lasted nearly 60 years and has yet to lose its appeal. The scenery has changed a bit, traffic is more of an issue, the car they drive isn't as cool, and they aren't young anymore, but it still feels like dating to them.

Don came from a family that was strong in their Catholic faith. After all, Don's sister and only sibling Rosemary had entered the convent to become a nun at the early age of sixteen. Don was active in his church as were his parents. He regularly attended mass at his parish, St.Henry in Rogers Park. This was the same church that Andrea had visited back in seventh grade to witness the marriage of her teacher. Andrea began attending mass with Don. She was not raised Catholic, but with Don being devoted to the church, Andrea decided to convert. So, at the age of twenty, Andrea made her first communion and confirmation, and the young couple continued to see each other nearly every day.

'My senior year at Lake View was very special. We dated regularly and Don took me to the senior prom. I felt so special. Sometimes we double dated. Dolores would go out with one of Don's friends and the four of us would go to a special place. One of those places was the Edgewater Beach Hotel where we danced under the stars to the music of Xavier Cugat. That was when Lake Michigan came right up to the back of the hotel, almost to Sheridan Road and Bryn Mawr.

When Rosemary decided to join the convent, we would drive out once a month to the mother house in Donaldson Indiana to visit. Then we would go out to eat at Mrs. Bennett's Chicken House. There were also many activities with the Luxembourg Club, which Don's family were long time members. Don's grandfather was an immigrant from Luxembourg.

Those dates were getting 'steamy' with all that togetherness.
We used to neck in the hallway on Reta Street and really steam
up the windows in the car. In those days, premarital sex was not
an option. We were both conforming to the expectations of the
times.'

Don headed off into the Service in 1953 which cooled
things off a bit. Rather than waiting to be drafted into the
Army, Don joined the Coast Guard. Eventually he was
stationed at the Locks back in Chicago which allowed the
two to see each other more often. As they were planning
their wedding and consumed in their own world, the tone in
the world outside was changing.

Fear of the Soviet Union and their growing military and
technological strength gripped the nation. An anti-communist
fervor was spreading throughout the country like wildfire.
Fueled by inflammatory accusations by Senator Joseph
McCarthy, hundreds of people were accused of communist
activities and many were subpoenaed by congress. Many
careers and lives were destroyed in what eventually became
known as an unsubstantiated witch hunt. The cold war was
underway. But Don and Andrea didn't have a care in the
world, they were in love.

The Wedding

✦

October 1954

Don's side of the family was big, having settled in Chicago way back in the 1890's. They resided in the same neighborhood, in fact on the same corner, where Don's grandfather had when he immigrated to Chicago from Luxembourg back in the 1891. The Luxembourg organization was large, strong, and thriving. And Don's father was right in the middle of it. Well into Andrea's golden years, she recalls Don's father's funeral procession in 1960 as the longest she had ever seen, before or since. It was nearly one hundred vehicles long.

Andrea's side was quite a bit smaller, having fewer family members and fewer friends. So she had entered an incredibly large and vibrant inter-connected community of people, always bowling, picnicking, or partying. Everyone knew Don's family, and Don's family knew everyone. Andrea saw Don's family commanding a level of respect from the community that her family had never experienced, and it blew her away. She felt important.

'We began planning for our wedding, which was to be in October 1954. Two very nice showers were given for us, one by my aunt Anna (Dolores' mother) and one by Don's aunt. It was a very exciting time. I felt lucky. We would have a small wedding with maybe a hundred people. But my father-in-law John had

many friends through the Luxembourger club and with those he knew for many years. Three hundred invitations were sent out.

My wedding dress was the first one I tried on. It was beautiful. There was a three-tier hoop skirt underneath, and a pearl beaded headdress with a long veil and a beaded purse. The whole outfit was $127.00.

We made arrangements to rent the Finnish Community Center on Lincoln Ave. It was a big hall and rental was $85.00. There was a 4 or a 5-piece musical group, which I don't remember the price they charged. Our food at the reception was a cold buffet which cost $175.00. Four hundred twenty five people were served.

As I looked out the window on that Saturday morning, October 9, 1954, it looked like rain. By the time I walked down three flights of stairs to the outside, the sun had broken through the clouds. It turned out to be a beautiful day. Everything went well. As I walked down the long aisle at Our Lady of Mount Carmel Church, with my father next to me, my eyes focused on my husband-to-be. It was hard to believe I would soon be his wife.

It was a special day. After the wedding mass, we drove to our family breakfast at the Luxembourg Gardens in Morton Grove. It started raining torrents by early evening and it didn't stop. The reception was crowded with faces I didn't know, except for a few on Don's side. My side was all family and familiar friends of many years. We danced, ate, and enjoyed ourselves.

We had planned to spend our wedding night at Hotel Moraine on the lake in Highland Park, but the viaducts were flooded due to the downpour of rain. We chose the North Shore Hotel in Evanston as a close alternative. The cost of the room at the time was $14.00. The next day we returned to our new home together, as husband and wife. We decided to postpone a honeymoon due to financial reasons and settle into married life on the first floor of Don's parents' house.'

Don's grandfather, JP, had lived in the house next door. Over the years before his death in 1948, JP had purchased the lots adjacent to his to give to his children. As a result of this, the family owned the last four houses on the block and the empty lot on the corner. Don was born in the big house next to the corner lot in 1930. The first floor of that house would be the young couple's new home. Don's parents lived upstairs. To this very day, Don and Andrea still live in that first floor flat.

A New Home and a New Life

✦

The morning after the wedding, Don and Andrea drove back to what would be their home for the next fifty plus years. The excitement of planning the wedding, and three years of courting was now over. As they settled in, and Andrea began giving the flat a woman's touch, Don went out to find employment. His Dad and he agreed on $75.00 per month in rent for the first floor flat, and a little leeway until Don got on his feet.

After years of exercising sexual restraint, as dictated by the church, both Don and Andrea admit to being confused, or even bewildered, at the new state of affairs. Just days before the wedding, Don and Andrea were obediently celibate, and living with their own parents. The day after the wedding they were living together as a married couple, just one floor below Don's parents, with all sexual constraints lifted. This was good, but a drastic change nonetheless that would require a bit of getting use to.

Andrea missed home and her mom and dad. Don was frantically trying to get settled in a career. They both felt pressure and a bit out of place. Andrea felt uncomfortable being away from her family for the first time in her life, and Don was worried and increasingly nervous about his ability to provide for his new bride. Andrea had never seen Don this uptight before. They were not less in love, mind you, but just getting a pretty good dose of reality. They were coming back down to earth. Married life wasn't what either of them had imagined.

'This is the stage of development when the young adult takes off the mask and tells the person with whom they wish to have an intimate relationship who they really are. I believe, in my case, this task was not achievable. The prerequisite to accomplishing this would first be to know who I was. Living up to the expectations of others, not questioning authority, and not being in touch with my feelings limited reaching the ability to be truly intimate. My 20's became a time of doing vs. being. All my energy was focused on doing for others. Being in touch with myself had to wait.

This was a time of change and learning new skills. Before our first child was born, I tried to get some sort of identity in inappropriate ways, by standing up to my new husband, like I was never able to with my father. It didn't work. I remember the exact place when I made up my mind not to argue again and remain silent. At that time it was the only way I knew how to get along. I was getting out of the car to see the doctor, to find out if I was pregnant with our first child. That was when I made a decision to keep the peace. Years later I had to unlearn that mind set for my own mental health and learn more appropriate ways to speak up.'

The couple had a new sense of purpose after learning of the first pregnancy. Andrea loved the attention the pregnancy brought from all the women in the family, and really started to feel connected. She had always had a high tolerance for pain throughout her life, so she was able to enjoy the experience of giving birth. Her first daughter was born in July of 1955; she was a good baby and was welcomed into the world as only a first born can be. The cost of the pre-natal care and the delivery totaled $75.00. Andrea's only regret with the birth of her first child was that her brother Bob wasn't able to see the baby right away and enjoy the experience with her. He had joined the army, and was being sent over to Germany the same week Andrea delivered. Hospital regulations at the time would not allow Bob to visit with his big sister and her new baby. Andrea had to wait to introduce Bob to the first new additional to the family in over twenty years.

Don was getting settled in a new position and a new career which served to relieve much of the anxiety in the house. Don and Andrea were really catching their stride as a new mother and father when the second pregnancy came. Their second daughter was born in October of 1956, just fifteen months after their first. This baby was born with jaundice. From this pregnancy they learned that their blood types were incompatible with each other. The baby needed a blood transfusion at birth. They felt fearful of the potential outcome, but everything seems to work out and the baby came home with the prospect of a healthy future. It was quite a relief.

Life was becoming a bit hectic when Andrea became pregnant again. Their third child was due in September of 1957, just eleven months after the last delivery. Don and Andrea started to become overwhelmed with the thought of having three children in diapers. Being devoted members of the Catholic Church, the couple knew that 'rhythm' was the only approved method of birth control. So they chose to follow the rules of the church, ruling out medically prescribed birth control, and did the best they could.

Three weeks before their third child was due, something went wrong. Andrea was out in the back yard hanging laundry as she always had, strung between the garage and the porch. She noticed that the baby didn't seem to be moving. She began to worry and had to wait for Don to get home. Remember that this was a time before cell phones and pagers. When Don finally came home from work, they called the doctor. By the time they arrived at the doctor's office, Andrea was already bleeding. The doctor confirmed their fear that the baby had died, and scheduled her for an immediate caesarian section and rushed her to the hospital. By the time they arrived at the hospital, Andrea was hemorrhaging. And by the time she entered the operating room, she had lost half of her blood. Andrea's own life was now in jeopardy.

Andrea survived after receiving more than a few pints of blood, but the baby was lost. In the confusion, uncertainty, and emotion of that day, their baby was never baptized, named, or buried. The deceased child was simply taken away by the hospital staff. Don took Andrea home two days later, relieved and exhausted. He was relieved that Andrea was alive, and relieved, in a way, that there would not be another child to care for. He was truly grateful that they had survived the ordeal together. They felt blessed and that God was watching over them. They dealt with the loss without dwelling on it because they had two young girls at home that needed their undivided attention. Life went on.

In July of 1958, only ten months after giving birth to a stillborn, Andrea gave birth again. Once a cesarean is performed, it would guarantee that any future deliveries would be by cesarean as well. So a baby boy was delivered by cesarean. The couple's incompatible blood types continued to affect their newborn babies. This child would endure one exchange blood transfusion at birth, and two more transfusions several weeks later. But the transfusions worked, making everything turn out fine. The baby survived, and Andrea and her new baby boy came home.

Shortly after settling in with their new baby boy, Andrea became pregnant again. Pressure was starting to build at a pace that was difficult for everyone. A baby girl was born in September of 1959. She was born underweight, at just over four pounds. This was Andrea's fourth successful delivery and fifth pregnancy, and the little girl needed two exchange blood transfusions in the first 12 hours of her life. But she made it, and became stronger and stronger as the months went by. The growing young family made room for one more. The total cost for this delivery was $1500.00. It was a far cry from the $75.00 they paid delivering their first child just four years before. Throughout their entire lives, at least until Don and Andrea reached retirement age and became eligible for Medicare, they never had medical insurance. They paid as they went, unthinkable in today's day and age. Back then, a catastrophic illness wouldn't bankrupt a family like it would today.

In that same year, 1959, Don's father, John, became ill with stomach cancer. John was without a doubt the driving force of the family, being very active in the parish and influential in the community. He had lived on that corner all of his life, since his birth in 1905. His father before him had been there since the 1890's. The family was established. John had dozens of friends and hundreds of acquaintances, everyone knew John and his family. Their house was very often a staging point for hunting and fishing trips, and the site for community meetings and parties. There was always a lot of activity at the house. On any given day, there was always someone coming or going for any number of reasons. This was Don's world, of which Andrea was now a part of. All that would change when John passed away. The visitors stopped coming by, and the phone stopped ringing. The parties and meetings went elsewhere, and the pace of life at the house slowed dramatically. The family not only lost its leader, but lost a way of life too.

Nearing death, John asked Don to care for his mother when he was gone. Don, honoring his father's dying wish, ending up living downstairs from his mother for the remaining forty-one years of her life, looking after her and caring for the family's property. Don was in his seventies when his mother passed away in 2001. So it was there, in the family's old house where the young family would stay. On his death bed in 1960, John told Andrea that she was the best daughter-in-law a man could have. For Andrea, it was the greatest compliment she had ever been paid. John's premature death was a shock to the family. He was only 56 years old when he died.

In the fall of 1961, Andrea learned that she was pregnant again. Another baby boy was born in March of 1962; he required only one blood transfusion to come home. This child would be the couple's last child. Andrea briefly describes this time in her life:

'I married at the age of twenty. My first was born in July 1955, the second in October 1956, a full-term still birth in September 1957, the third in July 1958, the fourth in September 1959, and the fifth in March 1962. I had four cesareans, starting with

a still birth, three in less than two years. At one point there were three children in diapers and the washing machine was going, sometimes seven days a week. It was a busy time, but one I wouldn't trade for anything.'

Even with the pressures of the first seven years of her marriage, Andrea loved that time in her life. Having little kids around was an exhausting joy for Don and Andrea. They took the kids out to show them off every chance they could. Andrea was learning how to cook for seven, Don's career was moving along well, and the kids were happy. The family had a big yard next to the house, and the kids made full use of it. Their first floor flat was only about 900 square feet, but they made due by utilizing every square inch. Don made bedrooms for the kids in the attic as well as the basement. The house was full.

Don and Andrea didn't know it, but there were dramatic life-changing events on the horizon. Those events would not only challenge their faith, but the marriage itself. Life for the young couple was about to become very difficult, but their unique combination of strengths would insure that they were capable of overcoming just about anything.

Tragedy and Breakdown

✦

1965

America was changing. It didn't seem the same as it was just a decade before. The war in Viet Nam was underway and civil rights conflicts were erupting in cities and towns across America. The young people were different than Don and Andrea were when they were coming of age just fifteen years earlier. Society seemed to be convulsing at every level. Hair was getting longer, the language becoming more vulgar and direct, and sexual expression appeared to have no limits. Respect for authority and personal restraint were vanishing before their very eyes. A great social chiasm was splitting the country in two, as young people everywhere were standing up to the establishment against war, social injustice, and suffocating social norms. Times were changing, but while the outside world was changing, Don and Andrea were raising their kids, paying the bills, and trying to get ahead.

The family was growing. Don and Andrea had five kids from three years old to ten and were very busy. It was a lot of work, but a lot of fun, and rewarding as well. The kids were healthy, active, and enjoying each other in that house on the corner with that big yard. Most of the other kids in the neighborhood lived in apartments with no yards and very little space.

Don bought a camera to take 8mm films of the kids and there was a lot of film, a lot of pictures, and a lot of memories in the making. Everyone on the block knew everyone else. It was a nice environment to raise the kids, they were safe and happy. Both Don and Andrea were very proud of their children.

They were happy, yes. But Andrea was exhausted. She was in a physically and mentally weakened state. When an individual becomes rundown, sickness in one form or another is nearly always close at hand. Andrea's overwhelmed condition would insure that any difficult event might become significantly magnified and any traumatic event even more so.

There are events in everyone's life that no one sees coming. A single event can change one's life, threaten one's life, end one's life, or shake one's life to its very core. There was such an event in store for Don and Andrea in the summer of 1965. It would determine the young couple's path for the rest of their married life. Or, at the very least, set their trajectory for years to come. Every family member and every dear friend would be impacted in some way, but no one more so than Andrea. It was an event that would ultimately define who Andrea would become.

It was a summer day. Andrea was in the yard hanging clothes on that clothes line strung from the back porch to the garage. The two youngest kids were in the yard with her, the oldest in the house, and the other two were in the alley with their cousins and other kids from the neighborhood. The children in the alley were lined up to get ice cream from the ice cream truck that came every week. It was a normal, carefree summer day.

Suddenly, Andrea's oldest boy who was seven years old at the time came running into the yard yelling and crying for her to hurry out into the alley. One of the kids had been run over. Andrea dropped what she was doing and ran out into the alley to see what had happened. She knew by the sound of her son's voice that it was serious. To her horror, she saw that their little cousin had been run over by the ice cream truck. It had accidentally backed over him, crushing his chest. The driver was initially unaware of what had happened, but only for a moment. The kids in the alley were screaming hysterically, among them were the little boys siblings.

Andrea's little cousin was lying on his back behind the truck in the middle of the alley. All the kids were crowded around him. She rushed over and knelt down beside him to try to comfort him and make sense of what had just happened. He couldn't move, but was able to look up at Andrea and tell her that his chest hurt. Except for the driver, she was the only adult in the alley and stayed with him until the ambulance arrived, talking to him and trying to keep him conscious. But tragically he died before ever reaching the hospital.

There was much confusion and hysteria in the hours that followed, but Andrea held it together. Even so, the effects on her and her family would last for years. She had held herself together at a cost. The emotional pain of watching a child die, a loved one so young, would have both an immediate and long term impact on Andrea. The pain was so great, and the need to comfort her children so immediate, that Andrea literally stopped feeling, blocking any emotion. She found herself unable to cry, or to share her grief with those around her. Instead she started to speed up, couldn't stop moving, and was unable to sleep. She had entered a 'manic' state, an extremely dangerous emotional condition. At one point the day after the boy's death, she took a magic marker and started to write. Not on a piece of paper, but on her bedroom wall, and wrote her way over the mattress and throughout the room. Before long the room was nearly completely covered in rambling scribble. She couldn't stop her body and couldn't stop her mind from racing uncontrollably. Andrea's situation was deteriorating rapidly.

At the little boy's funeral, Andrea was unable to show emotion in the midst of hysterical family members. People came to her at the church and praised her for her strength and apparent calmness. But Andrea wasn't calm; she was more completely overwhelmed than at any time in her life before, or since. She was nearing a complete collapse. In later years she wrote the following:

'In May of 1965 I was thirty-one years old, my youngest was three and my oldest ten. Everyone was in good health. There were no warning signs, physically or mentally and emotionally, for me, that would alert us to the abrupt changes soon to take place in our lives. Sometime in the middle of the month one of the kids, I'm not sure who, came running in the yard yelling, 'he's been run over by the ice cream truck.' I ran out to find our little cousin, only four years old, lying in the alley. When I knelt down next to him, he said that his chest hurt. He died shortly after.

The days that followed were very sad. I was the one who appeared to be strong, no tears seemed to come. But then something began to change in me. I started to go into a state of euphoria.

After a day or so, Don began to sense that something wasn't right with Andrea. He was grief stricken too, so hadn't noticed her condition right away. But after the funeral, it was apparent that something serious had happened to Andrea that day in the alley. When he looked into her eyes later that day he didn't recognize her. It was as though she had vanished. It frightened him more than anything had to that point in his life. Don immediately called the family doctor, the same doctor that had delivered all their children. The same doctor both Don and Andrea trusted so completely. They went to see him and he recommended that Andrea visit a psychiatrist. So they did. She continues:

The diagnosis was Acute Dissociative Reaction. I could no longer handle the reality of life, so I dissociated from it. I was admitted to Fairview Psychiatric Hospital. I stayed for almost a month. This was a difficult time for Don and my kids. Don had to make arrangements for all the kids to be cared for while he tried to maintain his own sanity. It must have been devastating for my kids to have their mother absent from their home and out of their life when they needed me so much.

When Don arrived at the psychiatrists' office with Andrea, he was in as dire an emotional place as she was. Between the death of their little cousin, the anxiety of placing his beautiful young wife in a psychiatric facility, his own employment situation deteriorating and facing unemployment, plus the responsibility to care for and comfort their five little children, Don was in bad shape. In fact, the entire family was in bad shape. Weeks later, the psychiatrist told Don that he didn't know which one of them to admit into the hospital, because he said that *'both of you appeared to need psychiatric help.'* Don then asked the doctor, '*Why did you admit Andrea instead of me?*' The doctor replied simply, '*Because you drove her here*'. Andrea continues:

'*While in the hospital, I felt as if all the fears denied over thirty-one years surfaced into one overwhelming fear which filled me with terror. It was night-time. On three occasions, I went to the nurses' station to ask permission to sit quietly by their desk so as not to be alone in the room. Each time I was sent back, the third time with a warning that if I returned, I would be put in restraints. Determined, I did return again with a chair which I placed near the desk. I informed the nurses that I had no intention of moving. I sat there all night. The next day, the doctor praised my actions and gave the nurses a reprimand.*

For me, the experience gave me a glimpse of myself I never knew existed. Suddenly there was confidence, the ability to speak up to authority figures, and to speak up if I didn't want to do something.

The world I entered exposed me to an exhilarating feeling of freedom and intense emotions. It was a world void of rigid control and high expectations. My strong will which had been suppressed as a child broke through to be acknowledged. These behaviors were praised by the psychiatrist, but considered abnormal for me. Feelings of fear and joy were intensified, making up for years of denial. Anger, an emotion I seldom felt or expressed, was absent.'

Before leaving the hospital, Andrea and another patient went out on a day pass to a nearby park with the consent of the hospital staff. The girl with Andrea was twenty-eight years old and hadn't spoken a word to anyone in months, and had been in that facility for several months. She took a liking to Andrea right away and Andrea to her. So the two made full use of the free afternoon and played together in the park as if they were little girls without a care in the world. They rolled down grassy hills together, laughing and yelling. They walked along the shoreline in their bare feet, shoes in hand. They laughed and talked together about their life experiences. They sat in the grass and made dandelion bracelets for their doctors. She told Andrea that it was the happiest day of her life. For Andrea, that day was a turning point, it released many years of pent up pressure.

Andrea's friend had spoken for the first time in many months. In fact, now she was talking to everyone. Later on, back at the hospital, the nurses asked Andrea what she did to get the girl to speak. Andrea simply shrugged her shoulders. Andrea and her friend had finally gotten in touch with the little child that lived somewhere deep inside of them. Well into her seventies, Andrea recalls that day with heartfelt gratitude.

Don and Andrea had always followed the rules of the church. Because birth control was not allowed, they chose to obey the directive of the church against their better judgment. That is, until Andrea's breakdown. They believed that having so many kids in such a short period of time contributed to their tenuous predicament. But they still needed approval before they would allow themselves to pick and choose which rules they could ignore. As with so many people of faith, they followed the law regardless of the personal consequences. They would finally receive the approval they needed, from their parish priest.

'My doctor said he was going to put me on birth control pills. I said that I was catholic and couldn't use birth control. Then our parish priest came to visit me in the hospital and gave me permission to go on the pill.'

Andrea learned from her stay in the hospital that she had a strong will. And that will, not being allowed expression in childhood, did not die, it simply remained dormant. She recognized this aspect of her personality as one that needed much attention. Years would have to pass before she was able to give her will a true and permanent voice in her life. There would be more to endure before she was ready and able to immerse herself in personal discovery.

The psychiatrist released Andrea after nearly a month in the hospital on a single condition: that she would not return directly home. The doctor felt as though Andrea needed a buffer, or vacation, before returning to her responsibilities at home. He suggested that Don take her somewhere for at least three weeks. He did. They arranged for the kids to be looked after, packed their bags and left. Not knowing where to take her and having limited funds, they loaded up the car and simply started driving. They would drive during the day and pull up to a motel in the evening. Unfortunately, the intended outcome to give her a break from her day to day routine and provide some rest for her didn't work as planned. By the time they arrived back at home almost three weeks later, Andrea's mental condition had plummeted.

Slipping Away

✦

Don was hoping that Andrea was cured, feeling better, or at least that the worst was behind them. Unfortunately, the worst was yet to come. She was still in a manic state when she returned from the hospital. That 'euphoric high' had now lasted for almost two months since that tragic day in the alley. When she returned home with Don after driving for several weeks, her manic condition quickly evaporated and sent her spiraling into a severe state of depression. Before long, her very life would be in jeopardy along with the fate of her family.

When Andrea had arrived at the hospital nearly two months before, the doctors started to medicate her. That continued throughout her stay and after her release. By the time she was back home she was taking seventeen pills a day and expected to pick up where she had left off. Not only couldn't she assume her domestic responsibilities, which by the way hadn't diminished in her absence, but she could barely manage to climb out of bed in the morning. Under heavy sedation and unable to perform any of her basic responsibilities, she began to feel inadequate, useless, and was pulled even further into depression and hopelessness. At that point, Andrea began to feel that suicide may be the only option, her only way to escape the pain.

In her own words:

'I began coming down from the euphoric high to a state of depression after returning home. Depression is about loss, it is anger turned inwards. It was a black period in my life.'

She thought of ways to end her life and finally decided that drowning herself would be the best way. So when she was alone in the house one afternoon she decided that it was time. She turned on the faucet in the tub and watched as the water level rose. When it was full she turned off the water and submerged her head. She held her breath as long as she could and expected that when she ran out of air she would drown. Well, after a minute or so she pulled herself out of the tub, choking and gasping for air. It hadn't worked. She had to think of something else.

Several days later in the psychiatrist's office, Andrea told the doctor that she wanted to kill herself. He never asked her why, just asked her how she wanted to do it. Andrea said that she had tried to drown herself, but that it didn't work. The doctor then strangely suggested that she try turning on the gas in the oven and sticking her head in there, thus dying of affixation. He said that might be easier. She agreed. The thought of a psychiatrist suggesting something like that today would certainly be cause for alarm. Yet maybe he knew that Andrea wouldn't go through with it, we don't know. But at home on the following day she couldn't bring herself to take her life that way, so her suicidal intentions would have to wait.

Months had gone by without relief. Every day she struggled to make the meals, wash the family's clothes, and keep up on her chores. All the while she was feeling hopelessness and was filled with despair. She was heavily medicated and felt as if there was no way out. As they had with the church, they also did with the doctors. They believed what they were being told and followed instructions. Finally with nothing else to try, Don and Andrea decided that the drugs they were giving her were making her condition worse. So they abruptly stopped the medications. Andrea was taken off all of the seventeen pills a day that were prescribed. Before long, she began to feel better.

'I was taking seventeen pills a day and couldn't even wash dishes. It was difficult trying to get out of bed in the morning. After five months of this Don took me to our family doctor, not the psychiatrist, and he took me off all medication. The depression lifted.'

As Andrea was coming down off the effects of the medication, her husband had purchased a book on positive thinking for her to read. It was as if they were inspired by the progress she had made after their decision to stop the medication. Don and Andrea began to take matters into their own hands. They decided to trust their better judgment and not blindly follow the directions of a psychiatrist. So she engulfed herself in this book and started to practice positive thinking. Every time a negative thought would come into her mind she quickly discarded it for a positive thought. Over and over again she repeated this exercise. As the weeks went by she felt better and better. It was becoming second nature for her to replace negative thoughts with positive ones. It was working. And with the lingering effects of the medication having all but disappeared she was becoming productive again at home. Even though the effects the previous six months had on the family would never go away, there was a tangible sense of relief. Don and Andrea and the kids put the whole thing behind them as best they could and moved on. For the kids though, their mom seemed better, but different in some way. She was there, but sometimes it felt as if she really wasn't. It was something that was difficult to pinpoint, but she was different.

Things started to settle down at home as many more months and years went by. Don wanted to believe that they had weathered the storm. He started to excel at work. He was winning sales contests, hitting his numbers, and making a respectable living. In the winter of 1968/1969 he even bought a brand new car for the family's adventures. It was a 1969 Pontiac Catalina Station Wagon and had plenty of room for everyone. The kids were in a variety of different sports and extracurricular activities. There were many evening rides to the Dairy Queen on Devon Avenue in Lincolnwood.

This was also a time when the oldest kids were becoming teenagers and venturing outside the family's protective circle. And Don was well aware of the changing and increasingly dangerous world outside their home. Robert Kennedy and Martin Luther King Jr. had recently been assassinated. Chicago was not immune to the protests and rioting that ensued. The Democratic Nation Convention in August of 1968 in Chicago revealed a societal instability that was reaching a boiling point between the races. It felt to everyone at the time that it could erupt into chaos without a moment's notice. Driving home late one night, after making sales calls in northwest Indiana, Don could see fires burning throughout the city from the rioting. People were running through the streets and he feared he might not make it home.

It frightened him to the point that it fundamentally changed his perception of the city and the safety of the country in general. This was not the place that he knew. He started to worry. He worried about the safety of his family. He worried about the intentions of others who may be influencing his kids. And with his oldest girls spending more time away from home, he worried even more.

Don's worry eventually turned into anger. Maybe it was latent hostility from the years the church refused them the right to use birth control. Where was the church when he needed them most? Decades before when Don was a boy, it was the parish priest who helped solve a family's problems. It was the pastor who always intervened on behalf of the family. Maybe it was lingering fear and uncertainty from Andrea's illness in 1965. Or maybe he felt that at one point soon his children would be out in a dangerous world without him to protect them. Maybe it was all of the above. Regardless of the source of Don's frustration, this was a difficult time for him. And any time a parent is uncomfortable, the entire family is as well. So life at home was becoming somewhat uneasy when 1972 rolled around.

Another Breakdown

✦

1972

The kids were growing up. The oldest girl was about to graduate from high school and the youngest boy was already ten years old. Everyone in the house had been affected by Andrea's breakdown, so life was different than it had been before. It felt as though no one in the family had ever really completely healed, but everyone seemed to be doing fine. Then the young family was hit again.

'In May of 1972, I went to a charismatic meeting at our parish. They were speaking 'in tongue'. Within a few days, I began going into a state of euphoria, with periods of hallucinations.'

Andrea didn't understand what a 'charismatic' gathering was when she agreed to attend. She didn't realize that she would see the same frightening behavior that she had witnessed as a child. This experience was as unsettling to her as it was so many years ago. Watching people talking 'in tongue' shook her to her very foundation. Before long, Andrea was drifting into a state of euphoria just as she had back in 1965. She was speeding up, becoming manic again. It happened that fast, with no warning. This time though, Don recognized it immediately. Literally terrified and not knowing how to stop it, Don put Andrea in the car and took her for a ride. He was hoping, praying really, that one of their long rides along with a little heartfelt conversation would help ease Andrea's worsening condition.

During the car ride, Don had to pull over the use a pay phone. He was supposed to be working and had forgotten to make an important call. He asked Andrea if she was feeling well enough to be alone for a few minutes while he used the phone. Andrea assured him that she was alright and would wait for him in the car. So Don went to make his call. But Andrea wasn't alright. And when he returned to the car a couple of minutes later, Andrea was gone.

Frightened and frantic, Don began searching the area yelling her name. Then from across the street, he saw his wife being dragged out a florist shop by some unknown man. Don ran across the busy street to find that the man who had Andrea by the arm was the owner of the shop. Don identified himself as her husband and took hold of Andrea. The man told Don that she had walked into his shop a few minutes before and started breaking vases, tipping over plants, and emptying shelves. The shop was all but destroyed. The man was as scared and upset as Don. As the three stood on the sidewalk, neither Don nor the owner of the shop knew what to do or say. Apologizing, Don offered to pay for the damages, explaining that his wife was very ill. But the shop owner, seeing Andrea's condition and Don's fear, told Don to forget about the damage and to just take her away. Sometimes good Samaritans appear when they are needed most.

Don managed to get Andrea in the car and back home. Her condition was such that he had to literally drag her from the car to the house, screaming, kicking, and swearing at the top of her lungs. Andrea had never used foul language. Their kids were all at home that day, watching these events unfold. With tears streaming down their faces, they watched as their hopes and dreams were disintegrating before their very eyes.

That evening, Andrea's cousin and lifelong friend Dolores came over to help. Don and Dolores had to restrain Andrea on the sofa so she wouldn't hurt herself. They decided that Andrea would need to be admitted to a psychiatric hospital again. Dolores was always there for Don and Andrea, throughout their entire lives. She always appeared in their time of need, regardless of what, where, or when.

The next morning, Andrea was admitted to the hospital and diagnosis was Manic Depressive Emotional Illness. While in the hospital, Don and the kids were reeling from seeing her in that condition. The kids were older and more aware now and more deeply affected by this breakdown. It was as if time was standing still. The whole family was traumatized, more or less in shock. Everyone was uncertain whether or not she would make it.

She was released a month later in a severe state of depression. This time the depression lasted for almost two years, so Andrea tried to keep as busy as possible to keep her mind occupied. The couple worked together to combat her depression. Don brought home books about positive thinking and self-healing. Andrea took a class to become a docent at Lincoln Park Zoo. But as she was approaching her fortieth birthday, the depression just didn't seem to want to lift. And then, help came in an unusual form.

One day, a friend of Andrea suggested that she attend a yoga class with her. Andrea agreed to go. While walking up the stairs with her friend at the first class, Andrea saw the others filing out from the previous class. They were all smiling, talking, and interacting with each other. And Andrea was wondering if she would ever smile again.

Once inside, the instructor asked that everyone lay on the floor, and began teaching the class how to relax. The lights were dimmed and soft music was quietly playing in the background. Andrea laid on the mat and before long, felt years of anxiety melt away. By the time the relaxation period was over, the black cloud of depression hovering over Andrea had lifted, and it never returned. She remembered her doctor seven years before telling her, *'the depression will go away when you find out what is wrong'*. A part of the solution to Andrea's depression may have been just as simple as that. She needed time for herself and time to relax, something that had been non-existent for more than fifteen years.

The simplicity of this revelation did not in any way minimize the joy and relief that Andrea felt from this breakthrough. She still had years of healing ahead of her, but this was the turning point in Andrea's life. In fact, it was a turning point for the family. Andrea was now released from depression and able to embark on a remarkable journey of recovery and self-discovery.

A New Beginning

✦

What a relief it is when depression lifts. Like having suffered from a raging fever that has finally broken, it feels as if you have been given a second chance. Hope reappears from nowhere. Andrea's dreams for the future are no longer simply prayers for relief; they are genuine possibilities of what could be. It was a new day and Andrea was given another chance. She embraced that opportunity as nothing she had ever embraced before. The past was far too dark a place to want to return. She was not going to let that happen again without a fighting effort. She had emerged a new person after more than a decade of struggle.

The country was changing too. The social upheaval of the 1960's and early 1970's was waning. The Viet Nam war had ended, but at an enormous human and social cost. Nearly sixty thousand American soldiers had died along with countless other Vietnamese. The president had resigned from office under an impending threat of impeachment, and the youth of America lost confidence in their leaders and their government. Sex, drugs, and rock and roll had gone mainstream, the lingering effects of the previous decade. This all was a far cry from the world that Andrea and Don knew as a young couple. Don and Andrea's children were coming of age in a very different place then they had known.

Andrea's yoga classes went on for eight years and she enjoyed each and every class. They gave her badly needed quiet time for herself. She could relax and empty her mind of day to day things. Yoga was essential to her new and healthy frame of mind. She was regaining her strength and energy, and she had a lot of both. Andrea still feared that the depression would come back without notice. Depression robbed her of all her energy. But the fear of an uncertain future never stopped her. She kept moving forward and never looked back.

Volunteering at the zoo and attending yoga classes were only the beginning of Andrea's recovery. Don suggested that she enroll in a class at Northeastern Illinois University, which happened to be only a few miles from their house. Although Andrea always felt that college was for smart people, and she had never considered herself smart, she did it anyway. It certainly couldn't hurt to try. So she attended her first class, English 101, at the tender age of forty-five. It was very difficult, but she applied herself without reservation. To her surprise, she not only completed the class, but she got an A.

She decided that she would try it again and the next semester took a class in General Psychology and another in Beginning Swimming. The psychology course opened up a whole new world of self-discovery for her. It allowed Andrea to begin understanding her breakdowns, or as she now refers to them, breakthroughs. The more she learned, the more she wanted to know.

She intentionally took the swimming class to confront her lifelong fear of the water. With some instruction and many hours in the pool under supervision, she lost her fear of the water. As her fear went away she became more and more determined to excel in the pool. And before her time at the university was over, she could swim one uninterrupted and unassisted mile. She could have never imagined such a day. The impact it had on her self confidence was clearly visible. In both classes, Andrea received two more A's.

These early successes motivated her to continue. She met so many interesting people and made new friends. Her world was expanding as was her mind. She had a new meaning in life and felt that she could accomplish anything. She couldn't wait to go to the next class or open a new text book. Andrea immersed herself in her education and loved every minute of it. It is safe to say that Andrea was on a mission.

After several classes in psychology she decided to make that her major. She also had begun classes in Twentieth Century History. The history courses gave Andrea insight into her youth and her times. She learned that there was an entire generation of people who had similar views and similar experiences. She was a part of something larger than just her personal experiences. There were many returning adult students at the university and she made friends with quite a few of them.

She also attended a course in Gerontology. She probably did so because her parents were nearing the end of their lives, or maybe because she always looked up to older people, or maybe because older people always treated her with such kindness. Either way, it was an unconscious beginning to many classes in that field. The gerontology prepared her for her working life after college, but she didn't know that yet.

People at the University were beginning to take notice and Andrea found herself being encouraged by many of her new friends, both students and professors. She was getting straight A's and found herself at the top of her class. After a couple of years at the university she had a near perfect grade point average. Andrea won a five hundred dollar award for 'Academic Excellence', and was selected 'Most Effective Speaker' in a speech class. She had found herself and found her stride. Each success ignited a more determined desire for more successes. She had found that not only could she be a college student, but she could be a really good one. She began to look beyond the next semester's classes, and eventually set her sights on a bachelor's degree. If she had made it this far, she could go all the way. The only thing that could stop her was fear of failure. But Andrea had no such fear. She had already shown herself that anything was possible if she tried hard enough. It would be a long road taking just a couple of courses at a time, but time she had. So she buckled down and gave the effort everything she had.

Meanwhile, life at home was changing dramatically. The kids were getting older and going their own way. Andrea's day to day responsibility to her children had diminished greatly and soon all the kids would be gone. Don was working from home as an outside salesman, while Andrea was at the university every day. She was making new friends and meeting interesting people. Don was slowing down and realizing that the business world would never provide him with great success or make him rich. He was never able to compromise his values in an effort to make more money. Don always had a solid moral foundation that was not for sale. He was never willing to relocate his family either, which limited any possible opportunities that may have come his way. He started to disengage from his work and wasn't trying nearly as hard anymore. It seemed as though Andrea's world was getting larger and Don's world was getting smaller.

Leaving So Soon

✦

The 1970's were giving way to the 1980's as the social landscape in America was changing again. The growing problem of illegal drug use among young people continued, igniting a national government sponsored war on drugs. The military had abandoned the draft for an all volunteer army. Eight-track tapes were replaced by cassettes and music videos. The VCR was leaving movie theaters only partially filled. The invincible American automakers were beginning to lose ground to smaller Japanese made cars. And the neighborhood that Don and Andrea called home was slowly but surely in decline.

Don was turning fifty and Andrea wasn't far behind him, yet both of them were in generally good health. Andrea's breakdowns were now in the past, never to return. This next period of Andrea's life would be about change. She changed the way she thought about herself, discarded the expectations of others, and set her sights on the stars. There would be no limits as to what she felt she could accomplish. While

Andrea was ramping up for an exciting new era, Don was winding down.

The household was changing too. The family was getting older, and one by one the kids were heading off into the world on their own. Where had all those years gone? It didn't seem possible that all those years could have passed so quickly, but they had. The kids weren't little anymore. By the mid 1980's, they were already all in their twenties and had moved out, with the exception of the youngest boy. All those years of sacrifice, struggle, planning for the future and worry were coming to a close. No more endless loads of laundry, or preparing twenty-one meals per day, or keeping them all properly clothed. It seemed as if it all ended in an instant, like it happened too fast to comprehend.

It had always been important to Don that his children receive an education. He stressed the point over and over throughout his life. He was intent on seeing that all his children complete a four years college degree. Most of the kids did so willingly. And in the end, all five kids earned at least a bachelor's degree in their respective disciplines. He felt it was his job to insure his children were educated, and they were.

As the kids graduated and eventually married to start a life of their own, they moved away from the old neighborhood. Most of the kids ended up living out of state. They were doing what was right for their own family's health and happiness. Don would not have his children and grand-children living on the same block as he expected, or at the very least hoped for. His kids were out in the world fending for themselves, out from underneath his watchful eye and away from his sphere of influence.

Don viewed these changes much differently than Andrea had. In fact, their opinions were so different, that it began to create problems for them and their relationship with each other and the kids. This was a time for strained relations all the way around. It drove a wedge of sorts, between the two. Don had grown up with family around him. When kids grew up, they weren't supposed to move away. They were expected to do what Don had done, stay close to home. He wanted to have his grandchildren nearby, just as his father had, and his father before him. His grandfather had made certain that his children all had a home on the same street. In Don's eyes it was the family's legacy. So when his kids chose to, or had to move away, it couldn't have come at a worse time for him. But the area had changed. Their neighborhood wasn't what it used to be. Once a great place to raise a family, now it was in a state of decline. It was no place to raise a family.

Andrea was in a much different place emotionally. She was happy and meeting many new friends, some of whom were men. This created some jealousy and strained her relationship with Don. The kids were moving away and Don was getting older. For him, this time in their life was a time when he seemed to be left behind, feeling in a way like he was no longer needed. It was a time of irreversible changes.

But Andrea had a different perspective. As children learn from their parents, so parents learn from their children too. She describes what she had learned from her kids as she reflects on them going out into the world;

'My oldest daughter has taught me how important it is to get dressed up, to feel good. During my 14 years at Northeastern I always got dressed up for school and continued that throughout my working years at the nursing home. That was a great tip. I also respect her good common sense, her wisdom and her ability to

adjust, even when it's difficult. She is a very special mother and a good wife to her husband.

My second has taught me how important it is to follow your dreams even if it causes conflict with others. We all need to learn and grow in different ways. She has always done an excellent job on whatever it was she was working on, and has done it her way.

My oldest son has taught me that our dreams and goals can be achieved in a quiet and unassuming way. He has always been able to have his needs met without confrontation. I respect that. I am also very proud of how he has dedicated his energies to being the best husband to his wife and father to his children.

My youngest daughter has a gift of giving and reaching out to others in need. Her spiritual growth inspires me and reinforces the need we all have to develop our spiritual side.

My youngest son has taught me that having a structure built on the belief in god, along with will and determination, can work wonders. He has also shown that addiction can be beat.'

Andrea found joy really, in watching her kids go off into the world. Her father had let her go when the time had come, so why should she do any different. She felt as though she and Don had prepared the kids as best as they could with what they were equipped with. She worried about the kids, having always known that her breakdowns impacted them, causing them to suffer far more emotional trauma then she ever had. She wished that her kids didn't have to suffer through those years, but for her, it was meant to be. She takes life as it comes without expectation. She has said throughout her life that one cannot control what comes in life. But one can learn from it and do the best you can.

Saying Goodbye to Mom and Dad

✦

Andrea's parents, Louis and Andrea, had moved down to Hot Springs Arkansas back in 1966. Louis had retired from the railroad and been able to secure a small home in a retirement village. The house was near several small lakes were Louis could fish. It was a beautiful place to retire, especially considering that they had rented an apartment in Chicago for more than three decades. He had also purchased a new Chevy Impala station wagon a couple of years before he retired to take down to Hot Springs with them. After all those years of hard work, struggle and uncertainty, Louis and his wife had actually retired in a relatively comfortable way. This was the payoff, the promise of America, the promise of opportunity and security for common people. America had held up her end of the bargain for the Schenks.

By 1981 it was evident to Andrea that her parents were declining quickly. They wouldn't be around forever so the time she had left with them was running short. Upon the suggestion by one of her professors, she went down to

Arkansas to spend some time with her parents to get their memories recorded on audio tape. Her professor said that it would be quite a gift to save those memories and also have the ability to hear the voices of your parents long after they're gone. So Andrea and her parents spent many hours together that week, talking about whatever it was that they could recall from their younger days. Andrea continuously prompted them with one question after another until the stories finally ran out. She had become a historian, documenting for future generations what would have otherwise been lost. It was an effort that she would appreciate years later. She found the effort to be fun and rewarding, and came to know her parents more intimately in the process. This motivated her to seek out and document more of their family's history in the years to come.

After seventeen years of retirement, Louis became ill. He had never been unable to take care of himself in all of his eighty-three years. But by the summer of 1983, time had taken its toll. He ended up in the hospital and then in a nursing home. His decline was swift.

Louis had been visiting his wife for some time in the same nursing home he had just been admitted to; he had long since been unable to care for her. So together they were being cared for in the home. Andrea and Bob went down to Arkansas to take care of the house and financial matters for their parents. With Louis unable to drive, Andrea ended up taking that Chevy station wagon back home to Chicago. It was her first car. She was forty-nine years old.

Louis only survived for a few weeks in the nursing home, and died in the fall of 1983 at the age of eighty-three. This left Andrea's mother down there alone, without her Louis. Over the next six years, Andrea traveled back and forth from

Chicago to Arkansas to visit her mother regularly. The years were flying by.

When asked about the time she was most proud of her father, Andrea replies:

'It was probably our vacations. The way he saved and planned was really something. We had a large glass jar in the kitchen with a small hole cut into the lid. Whenever we had a little extra money, it was placed in that jar. If I made money babysitting, or Bob made money on his paper route, some of that money would go into the jar. Dollar by dollar the money added up. My dad figured it would take about $250 to take that two month vacation. He would lay maps out in the apartment for months before leaving. He knew exactly what route we would take. I was so proud that that he took so much time and made such an effort to give us the vacation of a lifetime.'

When asked about when she was most disappointed in him, she replies:

'Dad had this pen that he kept in his desk. He used it to log his hours at work. He had always told us not to touch his pen. Well one day after he came home from work, he couldn't find it. He became angry when no one admitted to knowing where it was. Both Bob and I got a spanking that day. It was the only time in my life that he spanked me. I was angry with him because I never touched his pen. Decades later, when my brother and I were both married with children of our own, I asked Bob what ever happened to that pen. He finally admitted to taking the pen.'

Andrea remembers that her parents rarely argued in front of her. This made her feel safe and secure at home. Andrea never argued with anyone throughout her life because it wasn't part of her upbringing. When she was a little girl she used to walk her dad to the red street car stop every day during the summer to see him off to work. Those were fond memories, waving to her father as he boarded the bus.

In 1989 Andrea's mother passed away at the age of 89. *'Those bad memories'* of her younger days in Germany, that her mother never liked to talk about, had not revisited her in America. Whatever those memories were, Andrea's mother would never have to experience them again, because of her courage to cross the Atlantic Ocean and take her chances in America. She was betting that life in America had to be better than it was in Germany. And she was right.

In 2008, as Andrea was approaching her 74th birthday, she writes about the loss of her parents:

'I had good parents and now I have wonderful memories to last my lifetime. Mom gave me her love and taught me to believe in God. When I left the house she would say "now be good." Dad was reasonable in the rules I had to follow. I seldom heard him raise his voice. Dad loved to dance and I loved to dance with him. Just thinking of them now brings tears to my eyes. How I miss them. When dad died, there was no emotion, there were no tears. The same thing happened when my mom died, there was no emotion. Now I am in my 70's feeling the loss. Years ago my mom used to tell me that the older I get, the more I will miss her after she's gone. She was right.'

A Degree or Two

✦

Andrea's parents had passed on and her kids were leaving home all at a time when she had found a new meaning in life. She was embracing education and the exciting, electric, and youthful environment at the university. She had a new sense of purpose, a new yearning, and felt the exuberance of her youth again. It was a second chance at that lust for life that so very few of us experience twice. She was energized and engaged and coming into her own. And if anyone in this world deserved a new start, it was Andrea.

Her first few classes, along with her first few A's, gave Andrea some much needed and long overdue confidence. That confidence grew with each passing semester and each passing year. Throughout her life she had always avoided confrontation wherever possible. She did what was expected of her, more or less without complaint. In fact, her marriage with Don was more of a father-daughter relationship than it was a husband-wife, at least for the first twenty years or so. There was never a doubt, up until this time in her life anyway, as to who made the decisions around the house. But this was the 1980's, not the 1950's when the 'father knows best'. Now with her new found self confidence, this dynamic began to change in both her private life as a wife and a mother, and in her public life as a student. Andrea decided to do just as the psychiatrist told her to do.

There were new struggles at home. She no longer went along with all of Don's decisions. His decisions were regularly being questioned now, especially when it came to the kids. Andrea was in the mindset that their children had been given all that they needed to go out into the world. They would have to do the best they could, and if they needed help, Don and Andrea would gladly do what they could to help if they were asked. On the other hand Don wanted the kids to seek his advice before any important decisions were made. It was the difference between taking a hands-on approach or a hands-off approach with their kids. This created a rift of sorts between Don and Andrea. Neither could understand the other's position. The differences of opinions were growing between them, but Andrea decided that she wasn't going to be told what to do or feel anymore. She had always kept her feelings inside, but no more.

Such a drastic dynamic change within a household could, in many cases, cause a couple to irreversibly grow apart. And there were many difficult moments and equally difficult discussions that Don and Andrea had. But in the end, Andrea wanted her new experiences to include Don, and he wanted the same. Don would have to put aside his jealousy and extremely protective nature to make this work. He did, although at times, he did reluctantly. But above all, Don was committed to his wife who he loved more than anyone else in the world.

So he threw his full support towards Andrea's endeavors, and her successes grew exponentially.

Andrea's studies were progressing beautifully. She had completed a few classes in psychology and decided that this would be her major. Not only did she learn about her own mental illness (breakthrough), but she became fluent in the academic mechanics of it all. By 1984, she had been hired as a student aid in the office of the president of the university. For four years she worked in the president's office and came to know many of the employees, department heads, professors, and students at the university. Her world was exploding with excitement, new people, and new ideas. Classes in swimming, dance, film, women's studies, pop culture, 20th century history, jazz, art, the environment, race and ethnic relations, and humor in society opened Andrea's mind to an entirely new universe of thought and ideas.

She worked with handicapped students and the university to ensure the campus was entirely accessible to wheelchairs. Her growing list of friends crossed all boundaries of race, age, gender, religion, and socio-economic background. As she approached fifty years of age, after thirty years of marriage with five grown children, Andrea felt that her life was just starting. And it was.

She began writing a column in the schools paper called 'Professor Profiles.' Over the course of several years she interviewed some ninety professors and staff. Andrea knew many of the facility members and they knew her. She took great joy in meeting new people and learning about their likes and dislikes. She liked interesting people.

Andrea's newly found confidence allowed her to stand up for herself, not only at home, but at school too. There was one professor in a class that she was enrolled in that stated to his students that missing a single class was unacceptable. *'If you want to pass my course'* he said, *'you will attend all my classes.'* He went on to say that even the death of a parent was no excuse for missing a class. Well, Andrea had just missed one of his classes because of the death of her father. The professor, of course, did not know this. After class Andrea approached the professor and undauntedly said, *'You have a lot of nerve to talk to me and the other students the way you did. I'll never come to your class again.'*

Andrea had never spoken to another person that way before. She was sticking up for herself now, never to return to the old submissive way of doing things. She spoke her mind to more than one 'out-of-line' professor in her years at the university. All were appropriate, timely, needed, and done in Andrea's unique and gentle way.

By 1984, Andrea had been accepted for membership in The National Honor Society. In that same year, she was selected for the President's Award for Academic Excellence and the Promise of Future Achievement. And then in a culmination of her tremendous efforts, in 1986 Andrea was awarded a Bachelor of Arts Degree by the Board of Governors with High Honors, achieving a cumulative grade point average of 4.73. She was fifty-three years old. She had done the impossible.

Most people would spend a bit of time relishing an accomplishment of this magnitude. Considering where she was in life just fifteen years before, she had come a long way. But for Andrea, it still wasn't enough. For her to pass on what she had learned, she needed to learn how to pass it on. She enrolled in a Master Program in Guidance and Counseling. This was happening at the same time that one of her friends at the university had offered her a part-time job in social services to conduct support groups for the elderly at a nearby nursing home. She agreed to try it for a year because she wasn't sure she would like it. But Andrea ended up staying for ten years and loved her job. At the time, she had no idea how helpful this experience would be to her studies in the master's program. The graduate work went on from the fall of 1986 to the spring of 1993. Courses in family counseling, group counseling, individual counseling, and alcohol and chemical dependency were preparing Andrea to give back. She was on a mission, with complete confidence in herself, and in full stride.

Graduate coursework is more difficult and time consuming than undergraduate work. It took all the Andrea could muster to complete each class in her thorough and meticulous way. But she stayed with it even when she became overwhelmed. For nearly seven more years she ploddingly progressed through her studies with the intent of accepting nothing less than as close to a perfect grade point average as humanly possible. One success fed on another until she truly believed that she could in fact, earn a master's degree. Eliminating all distractions, she buckled down for the challenge of a lifetime.

In the spring of 1993 Andrea was awarded a Masters Degree in Guidance and Counseling. She accepted the degree less than a year shy of her sixtieth birthday. Fourteen years of hard work and determination had produced the most unlikely candidate to succeed in higher education and achieve academic excellence. At the ceremony and the festivities afterward, she was surrounded by her family. It was a day to remember, not only for Andrea and her family, but for anyone who has attempted to overcome overwhelming odds. Andrea had proved that anything is possible if you try hard enough. What a day that was.

The Tumor

✦

The 1990's had arrived and the country was on the verge of entering the longest period of economic expansion in its history. The condition and appearance of the country and its people was a far cry from what it had been during the Great Depression of the 1930's that Andrea knew as a child. Interstate highways now connected together every corner of the nation and strip malls dotted the landscape. Mass retailers and national chains were consuming the small and independently owned stores that typically give a community its flavor and charm. Customer service was changing from an attentive and appreciative owner to an 800 number directing your concerns to the unconcerned somewhere overseas. And as the land-line telephone began to give way to cellular technology, the file cabinet was giving way to the personal computer.

Chicago's north side had changed dramatically too, as the old landmarks which had come to be so familiar to Don and Andrea were disappearing from the landscape. The Edgewater Beach Hotel where the two had danced and dined as a young couple in love was torn down. Their long drives up Sheridan Road were no longer the secluded and peaceful rides they used to be as more buildings went up and traffic crowded the intersections. Angel Guardian Orphanage, an enormous complex of buildings that had defined the area for more than 100 years had been mostly leveled. The corner florist shop where Don had worked as a young man, and where his father had worked as well, was replaced by a gas station. And one by one, the old wooden frame homes in the neighborhood, just like Don and Andrea's house, were being sold, demolished, and replaced with condominiums and apartment buildings. A century had passed since Don's family had planted their roots in that north side neighborhood. But they no longer knew most of their neighbors as more and more ethnic groups moved in and started planting roots of their own.

Life around the house had changed. The kids were gone, yet Don's mother was still living upstairs and well into her eighties. Both of the family's dogs that had seen the kids off into adulthood had since died of old age and would be sorely missed. All of the other animals that the family kept for the kids through the years, the snakes and birds, ferrets and guinea pigs, cats and turtles, fish and iguanas, were all gone. But gone too was the stress and anxiety of raising a family, preparing the kids for adulthood, and planning for the future. The hectic pace and uncertainty of their middle years had passed. Don and Andrea were entering their later years, a new era with new challenges.

Shortly after being awarded her Master's degree, just a couple of weeks in fact, Andrea had heard that the university was offering free stress testing on campus. Andrea thought she would take advantage of the service and went in to get checked out. The medical staff put her on a treadmill and walked her through the evaluation. Everything seemed to appear normal and the doctor told her that she was in good health, with one minor exception. There appeared to be an irregularity in the blood flow around her heart. She was told that there was nothing to worry about, but to have an ultrasound procedure done anyway, when she had a chance, no rush. She of course felt great, had no physical issues, and passed the stress test with flying colors.

A couple of weeks went by before she went in for an ultrasound. Don was with her of course. Mid-way through the procedure the doctor found a very large mass, a tumor, right next to her heart. It was nearly as large as her heart, and appeared to be attached to the main vein feeding blood to the heart. They were in shock as they viewed the images with the doctor. Don asked him how serious it was and the doctor responded, '*This is urgent. She could be here one minute, and gone the next.*'

The reality of those words took only a few seconds to sink in, rendering anything else in the couple's life unimportant. Off to the hospital they went. Before the day was out, Andrea had already accepted the situation and felt no anxiety, no fear. She always had a high level of trust and believed that whatever will be, will be. Don on the other hand was terrified. He was terrified of having to put his wife's fate in the hands of strangers, of having no control, and of the reality that he might have to bury the love of his life.

Together they moved forward through an uncertain process. It appeared to everyone who was consulted that the tumor was malignant, it had to be. It was large and thought to be attached to a vein near the heart, so it was assumed that it was a fast growing tumor. There was no question that it would have to be removed. What was uncertain was who Don would allow to operate on his wife. He wasn't comfortable letting just anyone perform an operation on Andrea and he wasn't going to be forced to have it done just anywhere. He was determined to search and search until he found the person or place where Andrea's risk of death would be significantly reduced, or where he thought her chance of survival was best. The older Don became, the more he understood that doctors are human, just like the rest of us. And just like the rest of us, some doctors are good at what they do and others are not.

Finally, through a referral, they were able to send Andrea's information up to Mayo Clinic in Minnesota. The recent pictures of the tumor and Andrea's medical history were poured over by a team of doctors there and it was agreed that she would have the procedure done there. Don was in full agreement because he liked their methodical and patient approach. No one was demanding that an operation take place immediately, like everywhere else they went. He liked that they were considering several options on how to perform the procedure. He felt that this was the place and these were the people with whom he would entrust Andrea's life.

They had to wait several weeks before she could be admitted to Mayo. In the meantime, the two were going to pursue another suggestion made by a friend and faculty member at the university. Apparently there was an old Chinese man who had an herbal store in Chinatown on Chicago's near south side. Don and Andrea went down to Chinatown to pay him a visit. When they arrived, they were greeted by the old man's son and told him that she had a medical issue and was seeking an herbal remedy. The son led Don and Andrea into a darkened room where the old man was sitting. Andrea was asked to sit across the table from him, which she did. Then the old man gently reached across the table and placed his hands on Andrea's wrists. With his head lowered and sitting quietly with his hands on Andrea, he remained still for quite some time, as if in a trance. After a while he lifted his head, turned to his son who was sitting alongside of him, and spoke in Chinese. He told his son that she had a large tumor near her heart. But he said to tell her that he could prescribe a remedy that may help her. When Don and Andrea heard the translation they were dumbfounded. Don would later tell family and friends that he would have never believed a story like that if he hadn't seen it for himself. So they left Chinatown with a large bag full of twigs and herbs that they were instructed to boil into tea. Andrea did exactly that, three times a day, and every day until they finally made the trip to Mayo Clinic some weeks later.

Once they arrived in Minnesota, the doctors conducted some tests, took images of her chest, and prepared her for surgery. The surgical staff was able to successfully remove the tumor, and once removed, found it to be benign. They also learned that it was an old tumor, for it had been in Andrea's chest for many, many years. Andrea would make a full recovery. The sense of relief was overwhelming. Upon hearing the news, Don broke down in tears and hugged the staff with a release of emotion he had never felt before, or since.

Several days later, the couple went home to recover. Andrea would recover physically far more quickly than Don would recover emotionally. In fact the experience for Don would weaken him considerable, both emotionally and physically. But the couple did go home with each other, Andrea had made it. They still had each other, but came away from the experience knowing that time was no longer on their side.

Giving Back

✦

Back in 1989 Andrea had taken a job at a nearby nursing home that was to be a temporary position. She thought that she wouldn't necessarily like to work in what she believed would be a depressing place. She took the job believing that she would give it a try for a year and then make a decision. Well, the first year came and went, as did the next year and the year after that. Andrea found that it was far more rewarding than she would have ever imagined. The first few years of employment was a balancing act between work on her Master's degree and performance on the job.

Andrea had been doing her own thing for a while now. She had her own schedule and had very few distractions because the kids were of course, out on their own. The family had always had just one car until Andrea's father passed away and she inherited his car. The addition of that second car gave her the freedom that was essential to her new lifestyle. But her father's old Chevy wagon had worn out, it was almost thirty years old by then. So Don and Andrea set out to find a car for her. Don had seen a beautiful old car some years before in a grocery store parking lot. He put a note under the windshield wiper at that time, asking the owner to call him when they were ready to sell the car. Well sure enough, years later Don got the call that the car was for sale. Sometimes life provides nice little coincidences for people, and this was one of those times. The car was a 1972 Oldsmobile Cutlass, it was twenty years old but it was a beauty. Yellow and white with a black vinyl interior and was in beautiful condition. So Andrea continued to drive herself to school and work every day. Her studies and her work kept her busy and her self-sufficiency and new friends kept her happy. The years were flying by with hardly a notice.

With the Master's degree completed and having survived her first major physical health issue, Andrea focused on her duties at the nursing home. The longer she stayed the more appreciated she felt by the residents and the more she enjoyed the experience.

The nursing home had already begun holding discussion groups for the residents by the time Andrea was hired. Having a Master's degree in counseling, Andrea was able to apply what she had learned at the university to the discussion groups at the home. In fact, her Master's thesis was titled '*The Effects of Participation in a Reminiscence Group of Elderly Women in a Nursing Home*'.

Andrea found that it was very difficult to coax elderly women to disclose their life experiences in a group of their peers. Some of the women were Polish immigrants who fled Europe, or tried to flee but failed to escape the atrocities committed by invading forces prior to and during World War II. But over time, as the women became more comfortable with Andrea and began feeling safe within the group, they shared their experiences during their earlier heart wrenching days. One resident in particular, who was nearly ninety at the time, shared her stories of life in Poland during the occupation. Europe of the 1930's and 1940's had uncovered humanity's instinctual ability to fall into a dark world of ruthless barbarism. Andrea was stammered by what she heard. She had grown up in Chicago that no foreign army had ever invaded. She learned of the struggles of these women through their firsthand accounts of that time. Andrea came to realize just how fortunate she had been throughout her life. She felt that the difficulties she endured paled in comparison to what she heard in the groups. She was overwhelmed with empathy, gratitude, and a desire to bring some measure of joy and hope to the residents in her group.

There were good and inspirational stories too. One of Andrea's favorite residents was almost 100 years old. Every day in the spring and summer she would nestle close to her small television set in her room watching the Cubs game. She kept her note pad and pencil to keep track of the scores and statistics of the players. She had been doing this for decades. To this day it still amazes Andrea that a person of that advanced age could find so much pleasure in a baseball game. Andrea, as you remember, grew up just a couple of blocks from Cubs Park, so she could easily relate. She and Andrea became friends and shared their experiences with one another throughout her time at that nursing home.

One of the residents at the nursing home was Andrea's aunt and Dolores' mother. So Dolores was a regular visitor at the home as was her little sister, who was the flower girl at Andrea's wedding in 1954. This was a good situation for the three of them. Working in the same home where her aunt lived made Andrea feel connected, or feel that she was right where she was supposed to be.

The nursing home experience was rewarding and lasted many years. Andrea worked at the first nursing home for ten years. When that job was being eliminated she moved to another home for six more years. Starting at the age of fifty-five, Andrea worked for sixteen years in two nursing homes. But good things always come to an end, there are no exceptions.

By the spring of 2005, Andrea's working days would soon be at an end. One day, shortly after arriving at work, she was called into the administrator's office. She was informed that her position was being eliminated and that day was to be her last day at work. Andrea had been completely blind-sided and was crushed. She was literally in shock as she said good-bye to the staff and the residents. There were others who were crying. Andrea knew in her heart that her working days were over. She was seventy-one years old and starting the process all over again at another nursing home was not an option. This chapter in her life was at an end.

Some days passed as Andrea's new reality set in. And in Andrea's typical way she sought to find the good in the situation, just as she had done her whole life. She realized that just because she was no longer employed at the nursing home, didn't mean that she would need to give up all those relationships she had with the residents that she cared for so much. She was never a prideful or self-centered person. She could look beyond her unemployment for a greater purpose. So Andrea went back to the nursing home as a visitor, to talk to and visit with those residents who had come to depend on her for support, compassion, and love. The following week she did the same thing. And the week after that, again she visited the residents. Three more years passed and Andrea still went to the nursing home every week. She and Dolores continued their weekly visits to provide companionship for the residents. They continued to visit the home simply because they knew the residents needed them.

Saving the Family History

✦

Aside from the education itself, fourteen years at the university had taught Andrea that she could accomplish anything she set her mind to. She now had the research and organizational skills necessary to create complex documents. Having already received her Master's degree and only working part time at the nursing home, she had not only time on her hands but much left over energy from the years at the university. So she put that time and energy to work for her family. Andrea felt that her family had made sacrifices, especially her husband, so that she could attend school. So to take what she learned and create something unique for them would be a good thing. She also felt a need to explain what caused her illnesses and how she got better. After all, the kids bore the brunt of her hospitalizations, as did Don of course. They needed an explanation and hopefully some closure.

Her first work was a combination of two separate documents. First was a history of both sides of the family which she created without any research other than what had already been left by previous generations. By and large it included what was known about her and Don's parents and grandparents, mostly since immigrating to America. Andrea was wisely told by one of her favorite professors that if she didn't save that family information and put it in print, nobody would and it would be lost to history.

Second, was a chronology of events that led to her breakdowns, or as she refers to them, breakthroughs. All that she had learned through the years at the university about psychology, the stages of life and development as it related to her, and the course of her recovery were laid out in 'term paper' type fashion. It is well known that sometimes young children subconsciously assume responsibility for problems and trouble in their families. They might possibly enter adulthood feeling guilty, as if they were the cause of their family's problems. By clearly showing the actual causes of her illness and resulting hospitalizations, Andrea attempted to relieve the kids of any lingering guilt or confusion they may have still had from her breakdowns. She certainly couldn't take away their pain or reverse the impact it had on them, but she could certainly pass along what she learned during all those psychology classes.

Keep in mind that this was still a time before personal computers were in every household like they are today. So everything needed to be handwritten or typed. Andrea preferred to handwrite the information with her infamous fine tip felt marker, well known to family members and former professors. Written mostly in Andrea's unique style of cursive that forced the reader to move slowly across her handwritten lines, each page was a labor of love and very difficult to read. The markers she liked to use were not known for their conservation of ink. That being said, surely a few dozen markers were sacrificed for the effort.

Andrea prepared a large binder for each of the kids to present as Christmas gifts in December of 1995. Each binder was about three inches thick. In the last two pages of each of these binders, Andrea quotes the lessons she learned in psychology as it relates to her experience at that stage in her life, as a senior citizen. It reads;

The Final Stage of Life: Mature Age at 65+

Integrity vs. Despair

'In an aging person who has taken care of things and people and has adapted him or herself to the triumphs and disappointments of being, the fruit of all of life's stages ripens. It means a new and different love of one's parents, free of the wish that they should have been different, and an acceptance of the fact the one's life is one's own responsibility. In meaningful old age strength takes the form of accumulated knowledge, mature judgment, and inclusive understanding, which is all part of wisdom.Despair on the other hand expresses the feeling that time is short, too short for an attempt to start another life and try out alternative roads to integrity'.....Erik Erikson.

She continues:

'Don and I are coming around full circle. In young adulthood I was unable to communicate openly and honestly because I didn't know how I felt deep down. Consequently I was emotionally isolated. At this time in my life I can work toward intimacy in communication. It took me until my 50's to achieve a solid identity.

You can recover from mistakes in life by recognizing and accepting the lessons those mistakes provide. My surgery at Mayo Clinic at age 59 was meant to be. It was the only thing that could have slowed me down. Don's heart attack was a warning that he needs to realize that age is catching up and it's time to slow down.

This is a good time of life now. We are both healthy and still very much in love. The rides we have taken continue, it is our time now. We have always enjoyed being together and still do. Our appreciation of each other continues to grow. We have brought five special children into this world. We did the best we could. Now the rest is up to you.

As the years go by this Memory Book will have more meaning. Your children will know a little about their great-great grandparents. That is important to me that they do and I know it will be to you too.' Love Mom

The entire project took her at least two years to complete. Upon completion, Andrea felt a real sense of accomplishment but also felt as though what she created was gnawingly incomplete. She wasn't quite finished yet.

The way Don's family was established in their community and the sense of belonging that it provided Andrea seemed to evoke a feeling of pride in her. It was something that she didn't have with her side of the family. It became more and more important to her as the years went by. It may have been the frustration in her inability to get a real sense of her own family's history combined with the limited store of information available on Don's side. Or it may have been her need to hand down to her children something that wasn't handed down to her, something more extensive. Either way, she set out to undertake a task for her children that would take even longer to complete. The task wasn't something she was asked to do; only something she felt that she needed to do.

The idea to seek the information necessary to compile a family genealogy started with Don's curiosity about exactly where in Luxembourg his grandfather came from. A friend of theirs did an initial search and found that he came from Bergem, Luxembourg. This of course quickly triggered a desire to find out more, so Andrea set out to uncover as much about the family's history as possible. Over some 16 months, Andrea compiled Don's family history going back to the birth of his great-great-great-great-great grandfather in 1735 in Livange, Luxembourg. She was able to obtain birth, death, and marriage certificates from old churches and civil records and track the family's immigration to America. She could see nearly 300 years of family events being played out before her very eyes. She was quite frankly, fascinated. The more she uncovered, the more she wanted to know.

Finally, when the dead ends started to pile up, Andrea realized that she had gone back as far as she could without a significant additional financial effort. So she began organizing all the information so that she could create individualized binders for everyone in the family, and finally presented her findings to the family. Nine generations dating back to just after the reign of Louis XIV documented by microfilm records, were listed in separate texts she had prepared for each of her children. The earliest written record dated to the 18th century. It was well worth the effort, a rewarding and greatly appreciated enterprise.

The Last of a Generation

✦

When the last of a generation passes on it can be a sobering experience, or at the very least, a time of reflection. All of us who live long enough end up replacing our parents and enter our next stage of life as the elders. The transition really seems to take place when the last member of the previous generation passes away. We celebrate these milestones in our families, our communities, and as a nation. The country took pause when the last Civil War soldier died, as a community pauses when it's last surviving founding father passes on, and as families say good-bye to the last great-grand mother or great-grand father.

In the spring of 2001 Don's mother, Christine, passed away at the age of ninety-three. She had outlived Don's father by forty-one years, and had lived in that house since she married John in 1929. The first few years they lived on the first floor and then moved up to the second floor, where she stayed after John's death until her own in 2001. She lived in the same house for seventy-two years, just one year longer than Don, who was born there in 1930.

Don's father died early, in 1960. Andrea's father died twenty-three years later in 1983. And her mother passed away six years after that in 1989. Although Christine lived longer than her husband and the Schenks, she was actually the youngest of that generation, having been born in 1908. Her husband John was born in 1905 and both of Andrea's parents in 1900.

Upon her husband's death in 1960, Christine had to go back to work. She hadn't worked since she was teenager, employed at as seamstress, back in the mid 1920's. Needing an income in her early fifties, Christine took a job as an office assistant in a grammar school. She would get on the Peterson bus which took her to the El. From there the El took her down to the near north side and then a short walk to the school. It was in a tough neighborhood and Christine had her purse snatched more than once over the years. But she worked without complaint; she did what she had to do. She remained employed in that position for eighteen years until retiring at the age of seventy.

All the while, Christine lived upstairs from Don and Andrea. Her relationship with Andrea was always pleasant and mutually respectful. Christine never intruded into Andrea's life, even through the difficult years. She helped with the kids whenever she was asked, assisted financially whenever it was needed, and even made room for the kids upstairs when the family outgrew the first floor. Christine was generally a quiet person, but was really the anchor for the family after John died. Her presence gave the family a subtle sense of stability and continuity especially through the difficult years. Don and Andrea could have never come this far without her.

The changing of the guard didn't happen without notice. Don of course, had lived in that same house with his mother all of his life. But now it was just Andrea and Don there alone. The couple had married and moved in to the first floor apartment nearly fifty years before, at a time when the house was bustling with visitors, parties, meetings, and a lot of commotion. Now it was a quiet place and life had come full circle.

All the kids came in for their grandmother's funeral. The pastor at St. Henry was able to hold her service in the old St. Henry church on the corner of Devon and Ridge. It hadn't been used for the parishioners at St. Henry in decades. The archdiocese was using the old cathedral for other purposes, long ago having built another less opulent facility for the parishioners to hold their services. But considering Christine's history at the parish, they agreed to allow the family to celebrate her passing there. She had been baptized in the old church in 1908 and married there in 1929. In fact, she was the last surviving person at that time, to have been married in the old church.

This is an excerpt of the eulogy Andrea gave at Christine's funeral service:

'I met Christine fifty years ago when I was seventeen. She always included me in her life and family even before my marriage to Don. We attended Friday Novena together, bowled at the Luxembourg Ladies League, attended Easter Monday parties at old St. Henry School, and visited Don's sister at the motherhouse in Donaldson, Indiana.

During the forty-six years we lived in the same house we rarely had a conflict, we always seemed to get along. She taught me how to make a pie crust, broil chicken, yarn socks, and wash diapers. When her husband John passed away in 1960, Don was able to get her a job at the Board of Education as a school clerk. She worked from age fifty-two until she was seventy years old.

I'm grateful to have had a mother-in-law like Christine and to be a part of a family whose history goes back one hundred years in the community and in the parish. Our five children are the fourth generation living on Wolcott Ave. Last year we had a family reunion that included Christine's eight great grandchildren. Christine will be sorely missed.'

With Don's mother gone, Don and Andrea retreated to the old house to start the next phase of their marriage. In the last few years much of their time was spent tending to Don's mother. But now, for the first time in nearly fifty years, they were responsible for only themselves. And their house suddenly became very large. Don did the best he could keeping up the place, but everything was getting old and it didn't make sense to make things perfect anymore. Making broken things just work was good enough. Don had taken pride in the condition of the house throughout his life, rebuilding both porches, replacing the roof and chimney, gutting and remodeling both kitchens, etc. Even after his first heart attack at the age of 65 he kept going, maybe slowing down just a bit. But shortly after his mother's death he had another heart attack and it would be time to accept his age and slow down. So projects at home, at least the ambitious ones, were put on the back burner for a later time.

With Christine gone and the second floor empty, Andrea began cleaning and organizing the apartment for her own private space. It was after all a much more brightly lit flat than the first floor. With a large living room window facing south, the room was always bright and somewhat refreshing compared to the first floor, where the sunlight was always blocked by the building next door. They had never considered renting the flat. It just seemed like too much trouble. Plus, Don and Andrea figured that they would keep it available for Don's sister Rosemary, who still visited several times a year.

This was a nice time in Andrea's life for reflection and some peace and quiet. She hadn't had a lot personal privacy up until this point in her life. The upstairs apartment became her refuge. She had it organized as to her liking and had everything in order. She exercised every day up there, did her reading, and paid the bills. As far as it affected her quality of life, having the second floor to retreat to was probably one of the most welcome and appreciated events in her later years. She and Don after all, had raised five children in that small flat and had been living there together for almost a half a century. The extra space was a real relief for Andrea, and for Don.

Saying Goodbye to Bob

✦

Andrea's little brother Bob had raised a family of his own who were grown and on their own as Andrea's kids were. Bob had traveled the world fishing throughout his adult life, a love he had acquired from his father. When Bob and Andrea got together, Bob always came with photos and adventure stories from his last fishing expedition. In the spring of 2005 Andrea received word that her brother had passed away at home at the young age of sixty-six. Apparently he had been battling cancer for some time, but kept that from Andrea as not to worry her. She had no idea he had been ill. With Bob's death, Andrea was the last one left from her immediate family. This sobering reality brought on a type of sadness, loneliness really, that she hadn't felt before. She wrote the following letter about what Bob meant to her and sent it to all her children and people she knew. It was in a way a love letter to Bob, saying good-bye, and recalling memories of him.

'I Miss My Brother Bob'

'We always got along. I guess it was because we respected each other's differences. Bob was usually quiet like our dad. Many of my earliest memories are still vivid in my mind. We were living on Belle Plaine, Bob was about three years old, and I was about five. I just got the measles and mom put us in the same bed, pulled down the green shade so light wouldn't hurt our eyes. Mom said she wanted us both to get the measles at the same time to get it over with. We were in the basement with mom when Bob was riding a tricycle and fell head first into a coal bin. When he got up his eyes were black. Mom thought his eyes were gone. We moved to Reta Street when I was six years old in an apartment that didn't have any hot water. It took a while until dad had enough money to buy a water heater. It was a happy day for our family when he did. Bob and I loved turning on the faucet and getting hot water. The only heat we had in our flat was an oil stove which didn't heat the front room or the bedroom where Bob and I slept on bunk beds. Mom would heat bricks on the stove and wrapped them in towels to place at the foot of our beds to keep our feet warm.

Bob had a paper route when he was in grammar school. The newspaper had a contest and Bob was the winner of a beautiful Schwinn bicycle. That was an exciting day. And who could forget our wonderful cross country vacations in that old 1935 ford. Those vacations were why Bob loved to travel and go fishing. The years went by, Don and I married, and Bob went into the service. When he returned, he married and started a family of his own. We already had two kids when he returned from the service. I missed him when he was away and wrote him often. He told me later that he couldn't keep up with my letters. Bob was a good brother and good son to mom and dad. Our parents would have been so proud to see his home and garden and pool, *and to hear of all the exotic places he went just to go fishing. He learned early from dad.*

Bob called one day and said he was in the area and asked if I would like to have lunch. It was a memorable experience for me. Brother and sister, all grown up with families of our own, having a nice lunch together. Bob shared about his trips, what was going on with the family, and how his business was doing. We reminisced about our younger days. There was so much history between us that kept our bond so strong. I am very proud of that.

Months later I called Bob and said something I had never said to him before, Bob I love you. He didn't know what to say. Bob didn't want me to know that he had cancer. I found out after he died. During the time when he was ill, he sent me a large vase of flowers, no special occasion. I believe deep in my heart, that this was Bob's way of telling me that he loved me too. I'll always miss my brother Bob.'

As Andrea said good-bye to her brother, she was still looking forward to a special time in her life that was approaching. Don and Andrea couldn't quite believe that so much time had passed. Where had all the years gone? But their advancing years wouldn't quell their excitement for the event of their lifetimes. They would be the center of attention just as they had fifty years before on their wedding day.

The Golden Years

✦

The terrorist attacks of September 11, 2001 had propelled the country into a new era. The bustling prosperity, economic expansion, and excitement of the 1990's were replaced by the suspicion and fear of the new decade. The government began taking constitutional liberties to track down terrorists around the world that would have grave implications for freedoms at home and American status abroad. Don likened the emotional impact of the 911 attacks to the attack on Pearl Harbor almost sixty years before when he was in grade school. He said, *'This is what Pearl Harbor felt like.'*

The military invasions in both Afghanistan and Iraq contributed to a mounting financial crisis at home. Jobs were going overseas; inflation was on the rise, and a looming housing crisis would soon see more Americans losing their homes than at any time in American history. And during all the uncertainty and challenges of the new century, Don and Andrea went about their business believing that 'God's will be done' regardless of the disturbing events going on everyday all around them. They had made it to the turn of the century and fifty years together. Reaching a 50th wedding anniversary is a celebrated milestone in our society. Lifelong marriages provide an order and stability to communities that cannot be provided in any other way. In honoring these events, we honor an individual's ability to put the interests of a family ahead of one's own during times when sacrifice is needed most. There were without a doubt, times when it may have been easier for either Don or Andrea to just walk away from each other. There were times when it was more difficult to be together than apart. Marriage can be easy in the good times and nearly impossible in bad times. But it is in those bad times when staying together truly give marriage its meaning. Of course there are marriages that just won't work and everyone involved is better off when they end. But every now and then true love insures that couples will only part ways in death. Andrea and Don were the fortunate ones. No matter what had happened in their lives together, they both had reached this point with an undeniable sense of gratitude.

Time was flying by. They had long ago settled into a routine that met their needs and they both enjoyed. They continued their drives up Sheridan Road, mostly to visit rummage sales along the north shore. They would go out to lunch several times a week, sometimes trying a new restaurant, and usually sharing a meal. Though Andrea finds herself cooking at home more and more as the cost of eating out continues to rise. But that's fine with them because Andrea could usually prepare a nicer meal than they could find at any restaurant. It was a simply life without any great luxuries or extravagances. There was no mortgage to pay and taxes were low because of how long the family lived there.

Everything they needed was essentially within a few blocks of the house, with the exception of some visits to the doctor's office. They were more or less living off of Don's social security checks, and Medicare was paying the doctor's bills. As it turns out, the government had also kept their bargain with Don and Andrea, just as they had with the Schenks.

Life around the house was quite a bit quieter than it had been in past years. Just the two of them and their two dogs shared all that space. They always had dogs. When one died, another stray would coincidentally wander into the lives. The house was getting pretty old and the badly needed repairs were beginning to mount at a pace that Don could no longer keep up with. Andrea keeps the upstairs flat orderly and clean, a necessity for her daily retreats up there. So Don was more or less barred from touching anything up there, unless of course it needed fixing.

She reads and exercises regularly, keeping as fit as can be expected, but time and age had been taking its toll on her. So as she approaches her 75th birthday, she reflects on her life now: *'Being retired is a whole new way of living and has its advantages. Don and I can finally spend time together. We are lucky to still have each other after nearly fifty-four years. Our children are grown, the oldest is in her mid-fifties and youngest in his mid-forties. They have given us nine beautiful grand-children.*

It seemed as though my health issues started almost immediately after my working years had ended. A friend of mine told me that those health issues were just waiting for me to slow down before they revealed themselves to me. It makes sense because I really didn't have time for them when I was working. Nevertheless, I feel very fortunate to be in generally good health probably because of the good genes I inherited from my parents.

Exercise is an important part of my life now as it has been for many years. The older someone gets the more exercise is needed. If of course you are able. Don and I both feel pretty good, everything considered, and you can't beat that.'

When asked if he believes in a life after death, Don replied, *'I do. I believe in heaven and hell. I don't fear death and in a way I am anxious to see what is after death. I know my parents and my daughter who died before she was born are all in heaven. I want to know where they went. I don't believe that physical death is the end of me.'*

Andrea was asked the same question and replied, *'I believe in heaven, yes. But I don't believe in hell. How can a loving God make a place like hell? The answer is he wouldn't.'* Andrea continues,

'I was twenty eight years old when my nurse told me that the older I get the faster time goes by. At the time, that made no sense to me. I am in my mid-seventies now and very aware of how quickly the hours and days fly by. It must be because my lifetime is getting shorter. When I look in the mirror it reflects what aging does. But I had a good life when I look back. Sure there were many ups and downs, but that is what life is all about.

My faith and the power of prayer helped me through the difficult times. I do believe in guardian angels and when you treat others with respect, you usually will get it back. I have learned a lot in life. I believe that mistakes are lessons learned, and a negative can be turned into a positive. It is better to seek growth than perfection. Take care of yourself because getting old is challenging. My journey continues.'

From the Author

Discussions about the creation of this book began in September of 2007. I met with Andrea to begin the process of organizing the information and chronologies on a beautiful September morning. It was a day not unlike the day she and Don had celebrated their 50th wedding anniversary three years before. I picked her up and we drove down to her old neighborhood on Reta Street not far from Cub's Park. That morning we went from place to place talking about when she was young and locating all the places she lived and the places where she had played. It was a great and heartwarming start to this project. She was on cloud nine.

After a couple of hours of touring the old neighborhood we headed back to her house to sit on the front porch and discuss what we saw. Within a few minutes of settling in, she began to cough and couldn't stop. She had a relatively weak cough because of the pulmonary disorder she had inherited from her father. He had in fact died of that disorder. Her coughing was producing flam that had streaks of blood. Seconds later she was coughing up large chunks of blood. It was immediately apparent to me that it was coming from her lungs and not her stomach. As she tried to clear her lungs, the blood kept coming. She looked up at me in a way that I will not soon forget. She was scared, and so was I. She hadn't experienced bleeding in her lungs since she had fallen off the porch as a young child.

I quickly helped her to the car and we drove to the nearest hospital because Don wasn't home that morning. Before the afternoon had passed, both Don and Dolores were by her side. The bleeding did eventually stop later that day and she was able to leave the hospital the following afternoon. Apparently she was so excited to start the process of creating this book that her blood pressure soared to 200/120. The dangerously high pressure burst a blood vessel in one of her lungs.

During the ride to the hospital that day she clearly acknowledged that this could very well be the end of her life, right then and there. But she showed no sadness or regret, and even the fear that was initially evident in her face quickly passed. She was at peace with whatever the outcome happened to be that day. Her calmness and contentedness took me by surprise, in fact it startled me. I was far more upset than she was. It made me understand her enough to make this book possible. And after working with her over the next year, it all made sense. Andrea takes what comes her way. She doesn't try to control events or other people. She always looks for the good in things and the good in people. She expects others to do the right thing and simply accepts the reality of any situation she confronts. I have known her all my life, but the events of that day made me truly understand her for the first time. Whatever the circumstance, complaint and worry are never an option. We should all be so fortunate.

The Schenks in Kansas in 1910 (Louis on far left at age 10)

Andrea's parents in New York in 1929

Andrea at age 5 in 1939

On vacation in 1947 in the trusty 1935 Ford

Andrea holding one of the rabbits that kept the grass
mowed near Bowman Lake in 1948

Don and Andrea dating in 1953

Andrea a few minutes before getting married in 1954

Don and Andrea with all five children in 1962

Andrea receiving her Master's Degree in 1993
(photo courtesy of Loretta Downs)

Andrea in 2007(photo courtesy of Loretta Downs)

www.ingramcontent.com/pod-product-compliance
Lightning Source LLC
Chambersburg PA
CBHW051421280526
45785CB00003B/1104